Intrapreneurship
Handbook for Librarians

Intrapreneurship Handbook for Librarians

How to Be a Change Agent in Your Library

Arne J. Almquist and
Sharon G. Almquist

 LIBRARIES
UNLIMITED™

An Imprint of ABC-CLIO, LLC

Santa Barbara, California • Denver, Colorado

Library of Congress Cataloging in Publication Control Number: 2016038372

ISBN: 978-1-61069-528-2
EISBN: 978-1-61069-529-9

21   20   19   18   17   1   2   3   4   5

This book is also available as an eBook.

Libraries Unlimited
An Imprint of ABC-CLIO, LLC

ABC-CLIO, LLC
130 Cremona Drive, P.O. Box 1911
Santa Barbara, California 93116-1911
www.abc-clio.com

This book is printed on acid-free paper ∞
Manufactured in the United States of America

Contents

List of Figures

Foreword

Americans hold very favorable opinions of libraries and librarians. A Pew Research Center study in 2013 reported that 94 percent of those responding said that having a public library improves the quality of life in a community. Almost everyone—more than 90 percent in that same study—has visited a library at some time and has developed a perception of what libraries are about. This perception rarely envisions librarians as *change agents* even though librarians of the 19th century created the world's first true public library system. Librarians in the 20th century continued to build the public library system by innovating and making more services available. Their successors in the late 20th and early 21st centuries have used technology to revolutionize library services. Still, librarians are typically not recognized for fostering change, and libraries are not seen as institutions that have changed to keep pace with modern society.

In this book, the authors present the historical and contemporary case illustrating how librarians are indeed effective change agents, both within their libraries and within their communities. Within the change agent spirit, they explain the concept of intrapreneurship, provide examples of how intrapreneurship is taking place in libraries, and explain how all librarians can become intrapreneurs so that their actions may benefit libraries and communities.

The authors examine this topic from their experience in the field of librarianship and from their efforts as change agents and entrepreneurs. Sharon is an experienced instructor, having taught a wide range of library and information science topics to both graduates and undergraduates. She embraced distance learning models when they first became available and she has taught students across the country and in many lands using new technologies and new methods of instruction. She has studied entrepreneurship and managed a Media Library and established a multimedia lab that provided learning and experience for this research.

Arne has demonstrated intrapreneurship in his own library. As dean of the library at Northern Kentucky University, he has overseen a successful long-term effort to improve collections and services in the library. He has pioneered a new bachelor of science degree in library informatics to prepare students in Kentucky and other states for work in 21st-century libraries and other information-related fields. The partnership that he formed obtained two grants from the Institute of Museum and Library Services for training librarians and library staff members in Kentucky and West Virginia. This work has helped add professional librarians in rural and poor communities while educating many library staff members so that public libraries offer improved service—often using intrapreneurial ideas.

As State Librarian of Kentucky for the past nine years, I have seen firsthand the need for continued change using intrapreneurial concepts as described by the authors. The country's economic downturn in 2008 has resulted in many challenges for libraries. Like libraries in many states, Kentucky library budgets remain stagnant while the need for services continues to increase. Resources to support services for the public have become scarcer so decisions on where to make investments in service have become vital.

Kentucky's public libraries have proven to be good laboratories and learning spaces for the concepts suggested in this work. With new technologies available, library materials abundant, and staff who are open to new ideas, opportunities for positive change abound. I am gratified that the authors have chosen to highlight intrapreneurial libraries and librarians and hope that the examples will encourage libraries everywhere to embrace practices that foster effective and sustainable change.

Even though the public may not view librarians as change agents, librarians have made many changes through the years in order to survive—and particularly to thrive. Using the framework described here by the authors provides a route for continued change in order to improve services and meet the changing needs of communities. Twenty-first-century librarians would be well advised to study this book and incorporate its principles into action steps for their libraries.

Wayne Onkst,
State Librarian, Kentucky

Wayne Onkst served as state librarian and commissioner of the Kentucky Department for Libraries and Archives from 2006 until his retirement in 2015.

Preface

For many years the authors have been engaged in entrepreneurial efforts within and outside of their libraries without necessarily labeling themselves *intrapreneurs*. Arne, at the University of North Texas and Northern Kentucky University, worked to create an infrastructure to support and foster programs and projects and built a wide-ranging network to help leverage their impact. Sharon, in her role as head of the Media Library at the University of North Texas Libraries, constantly sought out new opportunities, such as her creation of the Multimedia Development Lab, which crafted interactive multimedia kiosks for the campus community in a pre-Internet environment. Currently, she is completing classes at Northern Kentucky University's Haile/US Bank College of Business toward an entrepreneurship certificate.

With decreasing levels of funding and increased competition, it is clear that there is a need for librarians to look at new and innovative ways of increasing impact, growing resources, and developing new ways of leveraging the unique skills and perspectives of librarianship to ensure that libraries are able to survive and grow. As managers, we encouraged, empowered, and supported our staff to expand their efforts, be creative, and to feel comfortable when suggesting change and innovation. Engaged in community service and outreach, we are dedicated Rotarians who fully embrace the Rotary mantra of "service above self" and are comfortable building and participating in partnerships that incorporate organizations of varying types and missions.

Like us, many of you are undoubtedly already intrapreneurs without realizing it. Whether you have changed an outmoded internal procedure, created innovative new programs to better serve your community, introduced fee-based programs to grow revenues, created or joined nontraditional partnerships to provide new services and reach new audiences, developed new technological innovations, or taken a chance (a calculated risk) and presented an idea for improvement, you have already displayed intrapreneurial instincts. Some of you may even be *accidental intrapreneurs* by becoming change agents without intending to do so because you saw a need and opportunity and took action.

Regardless of where you work, your position in the organization, your age, your gender, your interests, you can be a change agent and an intrapreneurial star at your library. This book is targeted at you: librarians in different roles and in various types of libraries, because change and intrapreneurship know no bounds. You will find the steps that any individual can take to be an effective change agent in her library, including how to get started, how to create partnerships and build networks, both within and outside of one's organization—and perhaps, more importantly, within and outside of the profession—how to handle difficult situations, and how to maintain momentum. From idea to execution, this book provides the information necessary to help you to become a successful intrapreneur at your library!

We would like to thank the many library intrapreneurs, often unsung, we have known over the years for their valuable service to the profession, but most specifically the founding librarian for the University of North Texas at Dallas library, now retired, Leora Kemp who selflessly offered guidance and support for this project. Many thanks also go to retired Kentucky State librarian, Wayne Onkst, for his collaborative efforts and championing of intrapreneurial enterprises in the profession.

We have written the book to be a (hopefully!) enjoyable read from cover to cover as you assume the role of change agent in your organization. The book can also be a useful reference to help you focus your thoughts and set goals and priorities. Use it according to your need and desire.

Arne and Sharon Almquist
Union, Kentucky

CHAPTER 1

Entrepreneurs

Entrepreneurship is neither a science nor an art. It is a practice.

—Peter Drucker[1]

An entrepreneur is someone who organizes, manages, and assumes the risks of a business or enterprise. An entrepreneur is an agent of change. Entrepreneurship is the process of discovering new ways of combining resources.[2]

Welcome to the world of intrapreneurship, an offshoot of entrepreneurship that is similar to it, and yet different in several ways. To better understand intrapreneurship, it is worthwhile to start our journey by examining the development of entrepreneurship and exploring the world of change agents, innovators, and the entrepreneurial mind set.

Defining an Entrepreneur

The word *entrepreneur* is derived from the French verb *entreprendre*, which simply means "to undertake or to begin something." Entrepreneurs are people who undertake an enterprise independently from and outside of any larger controlling organization. Similarly, intrapreneurs initiate change from within an organization. Both are change agents within their own environments.

Entrepreneurs have always existed. Most business entities or other initiatives begin with an idea and a person, or group of people, who turn that idea into a product or service that other people want to buy or use.

What Is an Entrepreneur?

> The entrepreneurial personality turns the most trivial condition into an
> exceptional opportunity.
> —Michael E. Gerber, *The E-Myth Revisited*[3]

As the term *entrepreneurship* became more widely known and used,
economists and businesses applied the general concept to specific
fields and circumstances. The term has become so popular that it has
been widely adapted and customized. Some of the adaptations and cus-
tomizations of entrepreneurship include the following:

- E-preneur—Web/Internet innovators
- Writerpreneur—using writing skills to produce an independent
  income
- Edupreneur—an intrapreneur working within educational institutions to foster and spread new ideas
- Teacherpreneur—teachers as intrapreneurs who continue to teach
  while fostering innovative practices
- Globalpreneur—"intrapreneurship within large multi-national
  companies"[4]
- Musicpreneur—performing musicians who manage their own
  business operations
- Bibliopreneur, infopreneur, or librarianpreneur—librarians who create new business concepts and sell products and services to libraries

The unifying concept within these terms is the diffusion of new ideas.
Entrepreneurs are, by their very nature, change agents and innovators. They embrace a unique way of thinking and looking at the world
combined with the ability to dream, create, pioneer, imagine, and
operationalize the dream; it is a state of mind. This spirit pushes an individual to be one of those people who visualize, create, innovate, and
change the future for the better—an entrepreneur.

To be most effective, change agents must know how to work well with
others. People who become drunk with the power of an idea to the
point of being monomaniacal defeat their own purpose. Truly entrepreneurial spirits believe in their idea, product, or service; however, they
know how to persuade, to excite, to convince, to plan, to implement,
to respect, to be humble, to listen, to retain a sense of humor, and to be
inclusive. Most entrepreneurs must work to convince others, such as

venture capitalists or angel investors, to support their project. Mainly, entrepreneurs are not motivated by get-rich-quick schemes.

Entrepreneurs need to work and play nicely with others, especially with those who may finance the entrepreneurial operation. However, Herbert S. White, distinguished professor emeritus, School of Library and Information Science, Indiana University Bloomington, laments the loss of the "old breed" of entrepreneur, those "rugged individualists, who will ignore the admonitions of others because they believe so firmly in their own judgements." White observes that these people may "frequently rub people the wrong way, in part because of their own low level of patience or tolerance for disagreement." He mourns this dying breed that has been all but wiped out by the need to conform, to submit to committee/team decision making, and to accept consensus.[5] Luckily the concept of conformity as it stood in the last century is losing favor in today's post-industrial society. Working and playing well with others remains a key component of the successful entrepreneur.

At a basic level, an entrepreneur is someone who tries something new, novel, or unique, generally with considerable risk, without the protections of a larger controlling organization. These protections may include financial and legal support or access to ancillary personnel. The entrepreneur's goal is to create a new product or service and to generate wealth. While entrepreneurs may make mistakes and may quite often even fail in their attempts, they above all seek to maintain a clear vision of their markets, customer needs, and expectations. Entrepreneurs make change and transform feasible ideas into marketable and profitable products.[6]

A popular conception of an entrepreneur focuses on a person who owns a business (including franchises) or is self-employed and operates a small business, such as a doctor, dentist, or plumber. Katz and Green make a distinction, however, between entrepreneurial businesses and small businesses. They characterize entrepreneurial businesses as truly novel in some way, while small businesses in general are often imitative and may do the same things as other small businesses with only a few differences.[7] For example, opening a new restaurant or dance studio is an imitative business. It is not life-changing or otherwise unique or novel because there are many other restaurants or dance studios available, often within the same geographic location. Creating a new computer operating system, such as Apple's Mac or Microsoft's Windows, is unique, novel, and life changing. Both types of endeavors, however, stem from someone, the entrepreneur, willing to take a risk, invest time, initiate change, and launch a new enterprise.

History of Entrepreneurs

How did these independent change agents receive the entrepreneurial label? The word *entrepreneur* became the label of choice for independent, risk-taking individuals in the 1730s when Irish banker and entrepreneur Richard Cantillon (1680–1734) characterized an entrepreneur as someone who created income that did not depend upon, or was guaranteed by, an employer. In its most basic form, Cantillon labeled any individual who took advantage of an opportunity to make a profit and to provide specified products to a defined customer base an entrepreneur. These entrepreneurs accepted some insecurity in both employment and profit because no one except themselves guaranteed either. In this model, those who worked for another individual, as an employee who received both guaranteed employment and remuneration, were not considered to be entrepreneurs.[8] They were employees. To make his point clear, Cantillon used the term *entrepreneur* over 100 times in his essay.[9]

Moving ahead to 1803, cotton manufacturer and entrepreneur Jean-Baptiste Say (1767–1832) suggested that an entrepreneur served as an economic negotiator who tied together the means needed to produce a product. These means would involve various people doing different things, who were brought together by the entrepreneur. For example, a successful entrepreneurial enterprise might be comprised of the use of one person's land combined with another person's labor, with yet another person's capital. The end result was a return on their combined labor or investment in the form of rent, wages, or interest for all involved. After paying the overhead, and the partners and investors, the remainder was profit for the entrepreneur, who had had the vision and vitality to bring it all together.[10]

Say also discussed how the value of a product may be established. He believed that a product's value was determined by those who used it, based on their perceptions of utility, rather than from the cost of the actual work or materials that went into producing it.[11] So the value of a car tire rested on the importance the person who needed to have it in order to drive his car placed on it. The value was decided by the utility he would gain from the tire's use, rather than from the individual cost of its elements, for example, labor and materials. Value is in the eye of the buyer or customer. If the customer sees no value in your product or service, then she may not be interested in it. End result: no sale for a product; no support for a service.

Assuming Say's product value to be true, how would his theory affect the value of library services? Just as with other products or services,

support for, and use of, library services would be based on user perceptions as opposed to the more traditional view of value based on the cost
of inputs, such as cost of parts or labor. Could this viewpoint lead to
smarter development of services based on meeting user needs? Could it
help libraries to better decide when a service was no longer needed or
when efforts should be shifted to a promising new service? All of these
questions are rhetorical at this point. As you examine each service and
its implications from an entrepreneurial standpoint, take the time to
consider answers to these questions. Questions such as these appear
throughout the book as food for thought for change agents.

Like Say, British philosopher John Stuart Mill (1806–1873), in his
Principles of Political Economy (1848), defined an entrepreneur as
someone who assumed "both the risk and the management of a business." While investors provided financial support and shared risks,
Mill drew a clear distinction between entrepreneurs and shareholders.
Entrepreneurs were the owner-managers who developed and ran the
business, taking on most of the risks while shareholders primarily
provided financial support.[12] Mill further noted that risk taking distinguished "the term entrepreneur from the term manager."[13] Here we find
a clear distinction between a manager, who oversees the day-to-day
activities of an organization, and the entrepreneur, who works with the
big picture and the uncertainties of promoting new products.

In a further attempt to define entrepreneurship in the 20th century, Austrian economist Joseph A. Schumpeter (1883–1950) introduced the term
creative destruction. Entrepreneurs, when examining markets and technologies, introduced new products or services that caused older products to disappear or to be destroyed because people presumably would
prefer the new and, usually improved, versions.[14] The world is full of
examples of creative destruction in which innovative ideas supply new,
and frequently unique, solutions to old problems. Microcomputers ren-
dered the typewriter obsolete while leading to the demise of the typewriter business of Smith Corona, a hallowed, long-standing company.
In turn, the PC market suffers in turmoil as newer, handheld technologies, such as the tablet, and cloud services have come to market. Recall
how the online catalog made printed card systems obsolete and how
cards made book catalogs obsolete. Note in the preceding examples that
the supplanting technology represented a break, or new direction, rather
than simply an evolution or modification of an older technology.

Schumpeter's view is of particular value to intrapreneurs because he
acknowledges that employees within an organization could be as innovative as entrepreneurs.[15] This is important to remember since he

viewed entrepreneurship as innovative, a way to initiate change, and the "process of doing new things and/or doing old things in a new way."[16] Schumpeter's discussion of entrepreneurs within businesses included what he called "dependent employees of a company, like managers, members of boards of directors, and so forth." Like Mill, Schumpeter described some entrepreneurs' progression into managers who, after they formed an organization, turned to managing its day-to-day activities.[17] What was originally a strength—making decisions without too much regard for others—became a weakness so that many entrepreneurs who were capable of founding enterprises could not stay to manage them once they became successful and mature concerns.

History of Entrepreneurs Supporting Library Efforts

What about innovative entrepreneurs who support library efforts? Those individuals who are not necessarily librarians but who seek to provide information or other library-type services to people who lack them? How have they gone beyond continuous improvement, beyond the sufficient and into the innovative? There are many examples of the efforts of these social entrepreneurs motivated more by filling a need than making money.

In 1851, merchant and philanthropist George Moore (1805–1876) funded a perambulating, or traveling, library in Warrington, England. It was a great success as each village had its own librarian and sub-scribers to the service paid one penny per month.[18] During the American Civil War (1861–1865) the Young Men's Christian Association (YMCA) responded to the need to provide reading materials to troops on active duty and those recovering in hospitals. The YMCA, through the U.S. Christian Commission of the Army and Navy, sent books and pamphlets to Union troops on land and at sea.[19]

Entrepreneurial women in the 19th and early 20th centuries ushered in a new area of support for their communities by providing books to those who lacked rudimentary library services. In 1897, the Kentucky State Federation of Women's Clubs appointed a committee for a travel-ing libraries project targeting people living in the many mountainous and remote areas of the state. Women from these clubs used their ex-pertise and contacts to purchase books and distribute them to people in areas without library services.[20] In South Carolina, Louisa B. Poppenheim (1868–1957), a graduate of Vassar College, felt that it was a woman's duty to provide support and take responsibility for her community. She emphasized principles of help and support over selfish pursuits, such as making money or garnering fame. By 1901, Poppenheim and her colleagues had donated 3,000 books to support free traveling libraries and negotiated for free transportation with the Southern Railroad in South Carolina. Poppenheim and the American women's clubs epitomized the entrepreneurial spirit as well as a solid commitment to their communities.[21] While they did not seek to make money from their efforts, these women did improve people's lives.

As we have seen, entrepreneurs without specific library backgrounds have produced innovations for the field of librarianship. Nowhere is this more evident than in the innovations of computer programmer Henriette D. Avram (1919–2006). Avram modernized the printed book and card catalog by recognizing the rewards that computerization of cataloging information could bring. She created the machine-readable catalog record universally known as machine readable cataloging (MARC), thereby making the location of library materials easily accessible through computer access. In 1970, the Library of Congress implemented MARC cataloging, and libraries throughout the world came on board in the following decades. A colleague noted that Avram, visionary and innovative, joined "the Library of Congress at a time when information technology and librarianship had hardly begun to intersect, [and] she immediately saw the potential of computers to create a networked global library catalog."[22] Instead of simply improving a known product, the card catalog, MARC revolutionized cataloging and precipitated the creative destruction of physical cards filed in a catalog.

Unlike Avram and other social entrepreneurs, information entrepreneur and linguist Eugene Garfield (b. 1925) made a substantial monetary return on his entrepreneurial activities. He founded the Institute for Scientific Information in 1960 based on his creation of citation analysis and bibliometrics. Another materially successful entrepreneur, Roger K. Summit (b. 1930), named the father of modern online searching, spearheaded the Dialog Information Systems at Lockheed Corporation in 1965. Both of these innovations greatly enhanced the ability to search and retrieve journal articles while at the same time bringing their founders monetary success. Both Garfield and Summit's innovations aided information science and resulted in lucrative enterprises, which contrasted with the innovations of social entrepreneurs for whom the success of their initiatives alone was their reward.

Another case of successful entrepreneurship may be seen in Africa, where the library entrepreneurial spirit has flourished by providing unique innovations addressing the needs of that continent. Undaunted by rough terrain and the lack of roads, the Kenya National Library Service invested in the Camel Library Service in 1996. Reading materials came with a portable tent library, a librarian, and two assistants. Stopping at village centers, the mobile library set up shop and was ready for business quickly.[23] The outcome of bringing books to those who had never had them was immense. In fact, the entire idea of bringing information to the users rather than bringing the users to information, through physical or electronic means, revolutionized library services.

Sustainable architect, entrepreneur, and educator, David Dewane, founded Librii in 2011 to build libraries in sub-Saharan Africa, a place where only 13 percent of the residents had Internet access. Each Librii library was a unique concept that offered a main building with study space and room for materials. Another area, fashioned from shipping containers, supported Wi-Fi and housed computers. Dewane commented that Librii was "giving the library a business model by balancing free and paid resources and providing a personalized learning experience, which ensures every dollar spent at Librii is having the maximum possible impact."[24]

Similarly in South America, teacher Luis Soriano saw a need and a way to share his own library books with children and adults in La Gloria, Colombia. Using his two donkeys, Alfa and Beto, he brought reading materials to remote villages through his Biblioburro, or the donkey library.[25] Outcomes were again achieved through a readily available process used in a new way.

Desert libraries, book mules, camel libraries, boat and train libraries, Internet access via solar-powered computers in a desert are all innovations that demonstrate the enthusiasm and passion that entrepreneurs on the periphery of librarianship exemplified when providing services in difficult circumstances. These individuals fittingly illustrate that the spirit of entrepreneurship is strongly embedded in serving library ideals as well as show the driving force behind social entrepreneurs, who rarely receive any monetary return for their efforts.

History of Librarian Entrepreneurs

As with those who supported library innovation from outside of the field, librarian entrepreneurs championed the profession while delivering significant innovations both as social improvements and those that made a profit for their founders. In 1843, librarian and professor of modern languages Charles Coffin Jewett (1816–1868) produced what was then a unique and innovative idea: a catalog of library books and pamphlets that offered access alphabetically by author. In addition to author access, Jewett provided an alphabetical index of subjects he created in order to offer the most convenience and detail to the users of the library.[26] Jewett's *Catalogue of the Library of Brown University* motivated Charles Ammi Cutter (1837–1903) to comment in 1876 that "Mr. Jewett was thinking more about those who are seeking information than those who are searching for a book."[27] Clearly, Jewett was forward thinking in providing not only access to a physical container of information, the book, but information about its pertinent details and location as well.

Cutter introduced his own innovation in 1880 while serving as head librarian at the Boston Athenaeum. Cutter unleashed on the library world a new form of cataloging called the Cutter Expansive Classification—not merely an improvement, but a radical change.[28] Cutter's system allowed books on similar topics to be arranged together and shelved next to each other, thereby introducing browsers to serendipity in locating similar items. Cutter's innovation was an important one in American librarianship, and his influence is still felt today. In creating a unique call number for an item, catalogers have long referred to establishing the author segment of the classification structure as "Cuttering." Although Cutter's system was not widely implemented, it paved the way for other systems of organization. Among them was Dewey's classification system, which eventually found greater favor in public libraries, while many academic libraries adopted the Library of Congress classification system.

Not long after Cutter introduced his system, the Library of Congress, in 1897, decided to establish a new classification system for its materials. Using Cutter's outline of classes as their basis, James C. M. Hanson, head of cataloging, and Charles Martel, who served the library as chief classifier in the Catalogue Division, established early editions of the new system. The system needed to be flexible so that it could not only arrange books on the shelves in a logical way, but evolve as new information was published and cataloged. The idea was to allow access to information through shelf order and considered subjects as "groups of books, not as groups of mere subjects."[29] This was clearly an innovative, and intrapreneurial, team effort. The Library of Congress classification system evolved internally over the years and based its schedules on broad categories of information, which were then broken down into specific disciplines.

Another American librarian and innovator, William Frederick Poole (1821–1894), originally conceived an idea for the first index of magazine articles in 1848 while a student at Yale College. He published the second edition of *An Index to Periodical Literature* in 1853, while librarian of the Boston Mercantile Association.[30] Poole tirelessly developed his index from idea to development to publication to revision and expansion. By the time of the third edition, much expanded, in 1882, Poole was aided by several other librarians.[31] Poole's index paved the way for the H.W. Wilson Company to publish the popular print resource, *Reader's Guide to Periodical Literature*. Again, continued innovation in the library world kept up with the pace of technology.

Positive outcomes and innovations continued through the 19th and into the 20th century. Consider librarian, scholar, and serial entrepreneur Melvil Dewey (1851–1931). Most librarians and library users remember Dewey primarily as the creator of the first narrow classification scheme for books, the Dewey Decimal System. Created while he was a student at Amherst College, Massachusetts, and introduced in 1873, Dewey was motivated to provide a system that, in step with public libraries, would allow people to informally continue their education after leaving school. He argued that an accessible, free public library was a way for people to better themselves and a useful classification system would allow greater access to materials. This is hard to consider in today's world of immediate access by keyword, hypertext links, and Google, but finding and organizing a collection of books in a meaningful and easily searchable way was an extreme challenge prior to the invention of this logical classification scheme.

When Dewey graduated from Amherst College in 1874, he received a temporary appointment to run the college's library as assistant librarian. At this time, he continued to refine and develop the classification scheme, ultimately applying for copyright. Leaving Amherst for Boston, Dewey entered into a business arrangement with Ginn and Company, an educational publishing firm. Dewey later founded the independent Library Bureau, which provided supplies, but not books, to libraries. The bureau's catalog from 1903 indicated that the company did not manufacture the products itself, but served as a one-stop shopping resource: "the most convenient, economical and satisfactory course when anything is needed for a library is to send directly to the office of the Bureau."[32] The bureau was an outsourcing agency for cataloging and consultation on legal issues, and provided an employment list.

These products included a variety of library products (see Figures 1.1 and 1.2), such as the two-tray standard cabinet.

Dewey's passion for libraries also led him to establish, with others, the American Library Association,[33] the publication *Library Journal*, and,

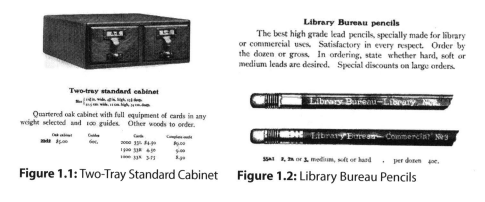

Figure 1.1: Two-Tray Standard Cabinet

Figure 1.2: Library Bureau Pencils

in 1887, the School of Library Economy at Columbia College in New York City. Dewey created multiple businesses and bureaus. In addition to the Library Bureau described earlier, he started the Readers' and Writers' Economy Company, which sold library supplies. Some of his business ventures failed while others succeeded. In the course of his business endeavors, Dewey combined the concept of public good with private enterprise and remained a driving force in the field of librarianship throughout his life. Wayne A. Wiegand observed that Dewey, like many focused entrepreneurs, "retained his boundless energy, intense commitment, self-righteous arrogance, and irrepressible reform spirit. He made many friends, and many enemies."[34]

Like Dewey's efforts at making money, one of the most famous examples of academic-library entrepreneurship occurred in 1967 when a group of Ohio University and library administrators established the nonprofit Ohio College Library Center (OCLC). Beginning with services for cooperative cataloging in Ohio in 1971, OCLC extended that service worldwide in 1977. The entrepreneur behind OCLC's shared cataloging system, Frederick G. Kilgour (1914–2006), served as a medical school librarian from Yale University. Kilgour had the vision to apply the newest type of information storage and retrieval technology to the age-old library concept of cataloging. OCLC has grown to become a major provider of library support services and remains a critical part of today's library environment. With revenues from library services reaching "$202.8 million in FY2015," OCLC remains a lucrative and major player in the nonprofit library world.[35]

Another example of an entrepreneurial effort that began within a library, but grew into worldwide prominence, was the VTLS online public access catalog system. VTLS emerged as a viable product when Virginia Polytech and State University's Newman Library could not find a suitable online catalog system and partnered with the university's

Systems Development to create one. In fairly short order, not only did they create a suitable system, but entrepreneur Vinod Chachra founded a for-profit corporation as a subsidiary of the university's Intellectual Properties unit. In 2014, Innovative Interfaces, Inc., purchased VTLS for an undisclosed sum. As with other entrepreneurial examples, VTLS illustrates how a local need inspired a product, which then expanded into a solution that solved the needs of libraries around the world.[36]

Like Chachra's efforts, the entrepreneurial spirit frequently lives within a library setting before it expands beyond and blossoms into a full-blown independent for- or nonprofit business. Such was the case with Peter McCracken, who, while a fulltime reference librarian at the Odegaard Undergraduate Library in the University of Washington (Seattle), started Serial Solutions in 2000, a company founded by librarians for librarians. McCracken noted, "The position of the librarian-as-entrepreneur is an important one because librarians know best what librarians need. The great thing about our product is it takes two to three minutes to explain to people what we do, and they say, 'Absolutely, we need that.'"[37]

Entrepreneurs: Why Do They Do It?

Entrepreneurship isn't simply about launching new ventures or making money. Instead, it's about solving problems and creating social progress; building great new things that make a better world. It's about celebrating each step toward the ultimate human longing for an enhanced and enriched enterprise of life.[38]

People may work for money, but they live for acknowledgement. By re-membering to thank the people who have offered you their time and energy, you make lifelong allies.
—Steven Schussler, founder of the Rainforest Cafe[39]

Monetary support is crucial to entrepreneurial success and that suc-cess often hinges on a team of investors, dreamers, and doers. Money is a key factor, but is it the only motivator? Frequently it is not. Many innovations begin in basements or garages with the entrepreneurs boot-strapping their way to success and profitability. Entrepreneurs pursue social innovations to make the world a better place. They feel a need to create, to achieve, and to meet new challenges and needs. Oftentimes, they make no money as a result of their efforts; their goals are focused on improving lives. Clearly, this view does not always fit the stereotype that many people have of the archetypal entrepreneur.

Anyone involved in a serious venture knows that money can make or break a project. It is often the key to moving from idea to the operating stage. So passionate are they about their idea that entrepreneurs often use their own money to finance their dreams and then pour any profits back into the development of their idea. Entrepreneurship takes focus, dedication, persistence, flexibility, and the ability to work in an ambiguous world. For many, the first idea, costing countless hours of work and great personal financial investment, is not the right one. The idea may fail, but the entrepreneur does not.

Librarians' entrepreneurial activities are often associated with those of social entrepreneurs who focus on societal change rather than personal or organizational profit. Social entrepreneurs want to make life better for people not well served by current systems. They create charitable and civic organizations that are self-sustaining. They seek out and secure funding. They create nonprofit, nongovernmental organizations that support charitable causes. They innovate and create workable solutions to seemingly intractable problems. They implement solutions through vision, persistence, and the promotion of their idea. They usually do not make money from their efforts.

In libraries and other nonprofits, the social entrepreneur frequently becomes the intrapreneur, expanding services beyond those currently or traditionally offered, by pursuing projects that may not require great outlays of time or money. When done in a collaborative environment, these efforts bring employees together to achieve common goals. For example, library intrapreneurs may seek to extend library services through outreach efforts that increase the library's geographic reach, open new markets, engage the community, establish partnerships, and expand clientele.

Entrepreneurs and intrapreneurs have always existed. As stated earlier in the chapter, entrepreneurs are people who undertake an enterprise independently from and outside of any larger controlling organization. Similarly, intrapreneurs initiate change from within an organization. Both are change agents within their own environments. Again, we find a close correlation between the entrepreneur and the intrapreneur mind sets: something to keep in mind as you read Chapter 2.

While we cannot always simplify, there are some basic differences between the goals and outlook of entrepreneurs, intrapreneurs, and conventional managers. Note that while Figure 1.3 illustrates generalized characteristics for the groups mentioned, and should be used for comparison purposes only, it is critical to remember that within the broader context everyone is an individual and a potential change agent.

Role	Entrepreneur	Intrapreneur	Conventional Manager
Growth	Future view Visionary Seeks growth and new opportunities for expansion of idea Looks beyond the status quo	Future view Visionary—future possibilities with resources from organization or additional resources through grants and partnerships Looks beyond the status quo	Current view Measured through available resources & outputs Content to oversee the current structure Generally upholds the status quo, but may support intrapreneurial activities when properly presented
Motivation and Rewards	Takes high risks for high rewards Financial success (or failure) Personal success: brought service or product to market Independent except for board of directors and shareholders (C Corporations) or other investors	Sees need for change in the organization, takes actions, devotes the time needed to process an idea Personal success: doing good in the community, improvement in services Rewards determined by organization through promotion, merit raises, and increased autonomy although never completely independent	Acquiring power Promotion up hierarchical ladder Personal success: recognition from organization Rewards through bonuses, merit raises, and across the board raises
Risk	Embraces high risks for high rewards Expects and believes in success	Accepts calculated risks Fears, but acknowledges and accepts, failure personally and for his or her team	Avoids risks Careful to negotiate through organizational policy Cautious
Failure	Makes mistakes Learns from failure, moves forward	Fears dismissal for taking a risk deemed a failure by unsupportive administration Makes mistakes and moves forward	Fears failure personally and for his or her team Fears dismissal for perceived wrong decisions Avoids mistakes

Figure 1.3: Entrepreneur, Intrapreneur, and Conventional Manager: Generalized Viewpoints

Decision Making	Hires PR people and marketers to help with decision processes Independent-driven by product or service Asks for advice from others such as successful entrepreneurs, lawyers, accountants, investors Seeks feedback from clientele	Skilled at selling his or her vision to managers and peers within an organization Quasi-independent—works within overall mission of organization Seeks feedback from clientele	Bases decisions on what the organization dictates and what the bosses proscribe Asks for input from staff, internal advisory groups, and outside boards, such as a Friends of the Library group Seeks feedback from clientele
Timing and Planning	Plans and sets goals showing 5- to 10-year estimated growth Embraces a long- or short-term strategy depending on the market Prepares a budget and business plan Creates personal sense of urgency Takes action	Sets time table to achieve goals within overall mission of the organization and organization's strategic planning document, 3 to 10 years Fits plans into overall strategic organizational structure Creates personal sense of urgency Takes action based on personal and organizational timetables	Plans based on organization's overall strategic planning document, goals, and timetable Decisions Makes decisions based on reports and budgets on weekly, monthly, quarterly, and annual basis

Figure 1.3: (continued)

15

Indeed, Say's theory of value comes full circle. Customers have needs. Needs determine value. Value spurs innovations. Innovations create products and services that meet the needs of a community. Entrepreneurs spearhead efforts to make the world a better place.

Like entrepreneurs, intrapreneurs want to make the world a better place; in libraries this means providing exceptional services and products. Chapter 2 begins the discussion of intrapreneurship and your place in the process.

Notes

1. Peter Drucker, *Innovation and Entrepreneurship: Practice and Principles* (New York: Harper & Row, 1985), viii.
2. Russell S. Sobel, "Entrepreneurship," *The Concise Encyclopedia of Economics* (2008), http://www.econlib.org/library/Enc/Entrepreneurship.html.
3. Michael E. Gerber, *The E-Myth Revisited: Why Most Small Businesses Don't Work and What to Do about It* (New York: HarperCollins, 1995), 23.
4. Matthew G. Kenney, "Globalpreneurship: The Need for a Line of Demarcation within Corporate Entrepreneurship Research," *Journal of Business Studies Quarterly* 1, no. 2 (March 2010): 4.
5. Herbert S. White, "Entrepreneurship and the Library Profession," *Journal of Library Administration* 8, no. 1 (Spring 1987): 11–12.
6. Jerome A. Katz and Richard P. Green, *Entrepreneurial Small Business* (New York: McGraw-Hill/Irwin, 2014), 7.
7. Ibid.
8. Richard Cantillon wrote the *Essay on the Nature of Trade in General* (*Essai sur la Nature du Commerce en Général*), a treatise on economics, around the 1730s (some experts suggest 1723 as a possible date, whereas others claim 1730); his work was published posthumously in French in 1755. It is his only surviving work. Cantillon also ran a business as a wine merchant. "Origins of the term 'entrepreneur' in English," *Law of Markets: Dedicated to the Economics and Politics of the Free Market*, http://lawof markets.com/2013/09/21/origins-of-the-term-entrepreneur-in-english/. In his edition and translation of Cantillon's work published in 1931, Henry Higgs discussed that all the people living in a country were either "undertakers" or "hired people" based on how they earned their wages (P.I.XIII.13). Richard Cantillon, *Essay on the Nature of Trade in General* (*Essai sur la Nature du Commerce en Général*), trans. Henry Higgs, with a new introduction by Anthony Brewer (New Brunswick, NJ: Transaction Publishers, 2001), 26. See also *Library of Economics and Liberty*, http://www.econlib.org/library/NPDBooks/Cantillon/cntNT.html. Higgs translated *entrepreneur* as *undertaker*, which meant a contractor who undertook work usually for the government.
9. Christopher Brown and Mark Thornton, "How Entrepreneurship Theory Created Economics," *The Quarterly Journal of Austrian Economics* 16,

no. 4 (Winter 2013): 407, https://mises.org/library/how-entrepreneurship-theory-created-economics. Brown and Thornton noted that "Cantillon's theory of entrepreneurship is that entrepreneurs function by bearing risk under uncertainty. They buy goods at known (fixed) prices in the present to sell at unknown prices in the future" (406).

10. Jean-Baptiste Say, *A Treatise on Political Economy*, trans. C. R. Prinsep, ed. Clement C. Biddle (Philadelphia: Lippincott, Grambo, 1855). Library of Economics and Liberty, http://www.econlib.org/library/Say/sayT.html. B. Janakiram, *Management and Entrepreneurship* (New Delhi: Excel Books, 2010), 141.

11. Jean-Baptiste Say, *The Concise Encyclopedia of Economics*, ed. David R. Henderson (Liberty Fund, 2008). Indianapolis, IN: Library of Economics and Liberty, http://www.econlib.org/library/Enc/bios/Say.html.

12. Sobel, "Entrepreneurship," *The Concise Encyclopedia of Economics*.

13. Peter Graham and Michael Harker, "Skills for Entrepreneurial Management," in *Entrepreneurial Management in the Public Sector*, eds. John Wanna, John Forester and Peter Graham (South Melbourne: CAPSM, 1996), 56.

14. "Creative Destruction," INVESTOPEDIA (2015), http://www.investopedia.com/terms/c/creativedestruction.asp.

15. Álvaro Cuervo, Domingo Ribeiro, and Salvador Roig, eds., *Entrepreneurship: Concepts, Theory and Perspective* (Berlin: Springer Verlag, 2007), 39.

16. Kenney, "Globalpreneurship," 2.

17. Cuervo et al., *Entrepreneurship*, 39.

18. Samuel Smiles, *George Moore, Merchant and Philanthropist*, 3rd ed. (London: George Routledge, 1878), 154.

19. Carrol H. Quenzel, "Books for the Boys in Blue," *Journal of the Illinois State Historical Society (1908–1984)* 44, no. 3 (Autumn, 1951): 221, http://www.jstor.org/stable/40189150.

20. Constance L. Foster, "Looking Back, 1976," *Kentucky Libraries* 59 (1995), 6.

21. Joan Marie Johnson, "Louisa B. Poppenheim and Marion B. Wilkinson: The Parallel Lives of Black and White Clubwomen," in *South Carolina Women: Their Lives and Times*, vol. 2, eds. Marjorie Julian Spruill, Jalinda W. Littlefield, and Joan Marie Johnson (Athens: The University Georgia Press, 2010), 111.

22. Matt Schudel, "Henriette Avram, 'Mother of MARC,' Dies," *Library of Congress Information Bulletin* (May 2006), http://www.loc.gov/loc/lcib/0605/avram.html.

23. Kenya National Library Service, "Camel Mobile Library Service in Kenya," c. 1999–2005, http://www.knls.ac.ke/public-library/camel-library.

24. Li Zhou, "Building Libraries Along Fiber-Optic Lines in Sub-Saharan Africa: The Washington, D.C.-Based Startup, Librii, Is Rethinking What a Library Looks Like," Smithsonian.com, February 23, 2015, http://www.smithsonianmag.com/innovation/building-libraries-along-fiber-optic-lines-in-sub-saharan-africa-180954192/#jmp7TTLzegIkJ8gE.99.

25. Simon Romers, "Acclaimed Colombian Institution Has 4,800 Books and 10 Legs," *The New York Times*, October 19, 2008, A5. http://www.nytimes.com/2008/10/20/world/americas/20burro.html?pagewanted=1&_r3&_r=0.

26. Charles Coffin Jewett, *Catalogue of the Library of Brown University with an Index of Subjects* (Providence, RI: Brown University, 1843), xx, https://books.google.com/books?id=ubFfAAAAcAAJ&dq=%22Charles%20Coffin%20Jewett%20%22%20brown%20library%20catalog&pg=PR20#v=onepage&q=%22Charles%20Coffin%20Jewett%20%22%20brown%20library%20catalog&f=false.

27. Charles Ammi Cutter, "Library Catalogues," in *Public Libraries in the United States of America, Their History, Condition, and Management* (Washington, DC: USGPO, 1876), 539, https://books.google.com/books?id=HC5FAQAAMAAJ&dq=%22Mr.%20Jewett%20was%20thinking%20more%20about%20those%20who%20are%20seeking%20information%20than%20those%20who%20are%20searching%20for%20a%20book%22&pg=PR1#v=onepage&q=%22Mr.%20Jewett%20was%20thinking%20more%20about%20those%20who%20are%20seeking%20information%20than%20those%20who%20are%20searching%20for%20a%20book%22&f=false. Special Report.

28. Charles Ammi Cutter, *Expansive Classification, Part I: The First Six Classifications* (Boston: C.A. Cutter, 1891–93), 4, https://books.google.com/books?id=AZgyIoIMs0EC&dq=cutter expansive classification&pg=PA4#v=onepage&q=cutter expansive classification&f=false.

29. *Report of the Librarian of Congress for the Fiscal Year Ending June 30, 1901* (Washington, DC: GPO, 1901), 234.

30. William Frederick Poole, *An Index to Periodical Literature* (New York: Norton, 1853), https://books.google.com/books?id=yO9GGjPbPjYC&dq=William%20Frederick%20Poole&pg=PP7#v=onepage&q=William%20Frederick%20Poole&f=false.

31. *Memorial Sketch of Dr. William Frederick Poole: From the Minutes of the Board of Trustees of the Newberry Library* (Chicago: Newberry Library, 1821), 7, https://books.google.com/books?id=DbcEAAAAMAAJ&dq=William%20Frederick%20Poole&pg=PP3#v=onepage&q=periodical&f=false. William I. Fletcher of Amherst College served as associate editor of the third edition.

32. Library Bureau, *Classified Illustrated Catalog of the Library Department of Library Bureau* (Boston: Library Bureau, 1903), 13, https://books.google.com/books?id=Jqw9AAAAYAAJ&dq=Library%20Bureau.%20(1902).%20Library%20catalog.%20Boston%2C%20MA%3A%20Library%20Bureau&pg=PA3#v=onepage&q=Library%20Bureau.%20(1902).%20Library%20catalog.%20Boston,%20MA:%20Library%20Bureau&f=false.

33. Miksa writes that if the American Library Association had followed Dewey's original plan "it may well have become a sizable business rather than simply a cooperative, not-for-profit, cultural organization. . . . In the

end, he failed to win approval for his corporate entity. And his failure essentially determined the first step in defining the Association's cooperative basis." Francis Miksa, "Melvil Dewey and the Corporate Ideal," in *Melvil Dewey: The Man and the Classification*, eds. G. Stevenson and J. Kramer-Greene (Albany, NY: Forest Press, 1983), 95.

34. Wayne A. Wiegand, "Dewey in Boston: 1876–1883," in *Libraries and Librarians: Making a Difference in the Knowledge Age* (67th Council and General Conference: Conference Programme and Proceedings, Boston, MA, August 16–25, 2001), ED 459 734, 8, http://files.eric.ed.gov/fulltext/ED459734.pdf. Wiegland is also the author of *Irrepressible Reformer: A Biography of Melvil Dewey* (Chicago: American Library Association, 1996).

35. OCLC, "Financials" (2015), http://www.oclc.org/en-US/annual-report/2015/financials.html. OCLC notes that it reinvests all of its "income into new products and programs rather than distribute funds to shareholders or business owners." Revenue from library services and investments "provide a strong cash flow that allows for strategic capital investments and to ensure the viability of OCLC."

36. John Pastor, "Entrepreneur Hall of Fame, Always Changing, Leader of Virginia Tech's First Spinoff Incorporates 'Vision' into VTLS," *Research Magazine* (Spring 2013), http://www.research.vt.edu/resmag/2013spring/s2013-chachra.html.

37. Norman Oder, "Peter McCracken: Librarian as Entrepreneur," *Library Journal* 126, 13 (August 1, 2001), 44.

38. Jon Burgstone and Bill Murphy Jr., "Why Entrepreneurs Do What They Do," *Inc.*, http://www.inc.com/jon-burgstone/why-God-loves-entrepreneurs.html.

39. Steven Schussler with Marvin Karlins, *It's a Jungle in There: Inspiring Lessons, Hard-Won Insights, and Other Acts of Entrepreneurial Daring* (New York: Unions Square Press, 2010), ix.

CHAPTER 2

Intrapreneurs

Intrapreneurship borrows from the principles of entrepreneurship. Whereas entrepreneurship is the act of spearheading a new business or venture, intrapreneurship is the act of spearheading new programs, products, services, innovations, and policies within your organization.

—Douglas S. Brown, Malcolm Baldrige School of
Business, Post University[1]

Definitions of an Intrapreneur

Like entrepreneurs, intrapreneurs have always existed in varying forms, but it was not until 1978 that American entrepreneur Gifford Pinchot introduced the term *intrapreneurship* in a paper he authored with his wife, Elizabeth. *Intrapreneur*, a contraction of the term *intra-corporate entrepreneur*, describes an individual *within* an organization who is an innovator and change agent.[2]

Entrepreneur Steve Jobs used the term in a 1985 *Newsweek* article published after his resignation from Apple Computer. Jobs said, "The Macintosh team was what is commonly known as intrapreneurship . . . a group of people going, in essence, back to the garage, but in a large company."[3]

As the term made its way into the standard management culture in the 1980s, many organizations, non-profit and for-profit, embraced the concept, that is, the concept of creating effective change through passion, perseverance, promotion, planning, and professionalization within an organization. These became key words to describe the internal change agent, the innovator, the intrapreneur. These 5 Ps as highlighted in Figure 2.1 epitomize the intrapreneurial mind set.

Passion	Look beyond the obvious for opportunities and ask, why can't we do something about this situation? How can we make it better? Passion means commitment to an answer. Remain engaged and communicate that to your colleagues.
Perseverance	Remain optimistic even if others do not see the opportunities you see. Understand rejection and turn it into a positive without becoming monomaniacal. Once approved, stick with the project no matter how many obstacles others may throw before you.
Promotion	Concentrate on creating value and bringing the solution to fruition.
Planning	In most organizations setting forth both short-term and long-range plans help to sell and promote your idea. Also set your budgets and goals with key targets that you feel are attainable. Do not over-plan. Do not allow persistent planners who are inspired by routine take over the process. Plan for success.
Professionalization	Be professional at all times in both your written and verbal communication. Remember that appearances do matter. Remain considerate and courteous to your colleagues.

Figure 2.1: Five Intrapreneurial Characteristics: The 5 Ps

The intrapreneurial phenomenon found its way into business, education, and library literature as evidenced in professor and entrepreneur Kevin C. DeSouza's explanation of the essence of intrapreneurship: "an individual's ability to be inventive and entrepreneurial within the parameters of an organization. . . . Being intrapreneurial requires a focus on commercializing ideas to arrive at solutions that customers value."[4] Commercializing simply means the process you take to turn your idea into a product or service available to your clientele. DeSouza additionally noted that while intrapreneurs could be—and in fact were—just as driven and excited about their ideas as entrepreneurs, these internal change agents elected to use their talents within their organization's structure while making use of their organization's resources.[5]

Intrapreneurs were further examined by Donald F. Kuratko, professor of entrepreneurship at the Kelley School of Business, Indiana University (Bloomington), and Richard M. Hodgetts, Suntrust professor of strategic management at Florida International University. Kuratko and Hodgetts clearly equated the concept of intrapreneurship with innovation. They stated that intrapreneurs receive "organizational sanction and resource commitments for the purpose of innovative results. The major thrust of intrapreneuring is to develop the entrepreneurial spirit within organizational boundaries, thus allowing an atmosphere of innovation to prosper."[6] The key point here is *within the organizational boundaries*. Those who dismiss and sabotage others' innovative ideas, work to disrupt the organization, or use the cover of innovation or intrapreneurship for their own purposes are pseudo-intrapreneurs or rogues. These individuals are not true change agents and in the end their behavior will have negative consequences for their clientele, the organization, and themselves.

Successful entrepreneur and author Guy Kawasaki further expounds on the organizational boundary point. Kawasaki, who was one of the intrapreneurs responsible for the success of Apple's Macintosh computer, devoted a mini-chapter in his self-help book *The Art of the Start* to the art of internal entrepreneuring. Kawasaki discussed how intrapreneurs' main motivation should be the improvement of their organization. Within an organization, intrapreneurs must display qualities that allow them to use finesse, diplomacy, and a certain amount of charm to sell a new idea to their colleagues. It's not about forcing your will on others. It is about persuasion and collaboration—both up and down the organizational structure. If your idea is a good one, others will support you, but only, as Kawasaki notes, "if you're doing it for the company, . . . not if it's for your personal gain."[7]

Kawasaki also noted that truly effective intrapreneurs keep track of new paradigms and hold ideas ready to address issues quickly. They are people who are proactive, not reactive. They are the ones who walk into the boss's office and say, "Hey, I've got this idea." They question, but more importantly they offer solutions. They work with, not around or through, others. They are optimistic, not negative. They cultivate ideas and their colleagues. Ask yourself: Do you keep abreast of current developments in technology? In your community? In library trends? Do you really see what you can offer your clientele? Are you willing to support your colleagues in a new effort that can really improve services? Are you collegial? Are you willing to keep your great idea in check until the time is ripe for commercialization?

Remaining proactive and engaged leads not only to personal organizational success, but to personal satisfaction and a positive work environment. Manipulative tactics, such as bullying, going it alone, destructive criticism, and whispering campaigns, have no place in an innovative workplace. No one should underestimate or demean the value and abilities of a fellow employee, manager, or even the big boss. The excuse that "she's too old to really understand technology" or "I just don't agree with this project so I'll not support it" degrades the entire intrapreneurial process. Remember that it is up to you, the intrapreneur, to generate excitement for your innovations and ensure that people at all levels and ages are capable of becoming meaningful intrapreneurs.[8] One size does not fit all.

Not surprisingly, as librarians embrace the concept of intrapreneurship, and even recognize themselves as intrapreneurs, they have promoted the concept through conferences and webinars. In 2009 the first Entrelib: The Conference for Entrepreneurial Librarians was held, promoting internal change agents through conferences and webinars. In 2014, the conference focused on risks and change and in 2016 enticed innovators with the conference title "Imagine the NEXT!"[9]

The environments of entrepreneurs and intrapreneurs are different. Intrapreneurs choose to stay within an organization; they have stability in terms of job and pay; they do not need to put their own finances on the line to launch a new product or service. That said, intrapreneurs contribute their own time and may put their reputations on the line to advance a change they truly believe in and one that fits into the framework of their organization. Indeed, intrapreneurship can lead to increased job satisfaction for those who embrace it. Matthew G. Kenney, writing about academic entrepreneurship and faculty job satisfaction, notes that "experienced academicians are increasingly more interested in pursuing innovative career opportunities as it leads to increased recognition in their field." Engaged and satisfied employees create greater stability in the organization as well as greater innovation.[10]

Enter the intrapreneur: a change agent who shares many of the characteristics and motivations of an entrepreneur, but who works within a large or small institution and relies on that organization for financial remuneration and organizational support. Motivationally, both intrapreneurs and entrepreneurs are driven more by a passion to create rather than by the desire to make more money. For librarians and others working in libraries, establishing new services within the structure of their organizations, and, perhaps more importantly, envisioning creative ways of applying their unique perspectives and skills in an expanding context reflects this creative zeal.

Certainly, with the rise of a global economy, immediate access to knowledge and communications, and the rise of for-profit and non-profit competitors, library intrapreneurs are revising old services and doing many things in new ways. Continuous innovation is the key to success, especially in large organizations that can become bogged down in bureaucratic red tape and cannot adapt quickly. Even while legacy services are being maintained, innovators can pursue new ways and means of providing services (see Figure 2.2).

The Diamond Law Library at the Columbia Law School provides an example of an access fee–based service. Upon payment of suitable fees, the library offers those outside of their standard clientele access to several important collections, a document delivery pay-as-you-go service, and a subscription service allowing local subscribers who pay an annual fee, such as law firms or companies, access to the law library collections and other privileges.[12] Other traditional sources of library fees include rental of rooms, sales of withdrawn books and other materials, photocopy charges, sale of digital storage media, and access to specialized services or databases.

Not all fee-based services are successful or even marginally cost effective. Where benefits are not evident, services can and should be discontinued. In the early 1990s, the library at the University of Hartford, Connecticut, conducted market research and pilot projects and decided to launch a fee-based electronic information service called Corporate Information Services for off-campus clients. The monetary investment in the project did not merit its continuation and the library cancelled the service after just two years. While perseverance is a good trait in an entrepreneur, mistakes are made and it is admirable to recognize those mistakes and correct them, sometimes by terminating an idea and moving on.[13]

Still, some extra money can be a welcome outcome. When Mindy Reed, a librarian at the Austin (Texas) Public Library, created a permanent bookstore and upcycling facility called Recycled Reads, she implemented new and innovative uses for discarded library books.

Kyle Courtney, Harvard University's copyright advisor, received a *Library Journal* 2015 Movers and Shakers Change Agent Award. He embodied the soul of the intrapreneur in his response to the question: "What three tips would you give to potential Movers & Shakers?

1. Never give up on your vision.
2. Talk to your colleagues, peers, and friends. Have a bunch of people you can bounce ideas off of.
3. Do what you love. My passion for this has helped drive me through times when it's a lot of work—if you do what you love, it doesn't feel so much like work."

Figure 2.2: Change Agent in Action[11]

Reed, a recipient of the Movers and Shakers 2015 Innovators Award from *Library Journal*, based her idea on the simple question of how to do something better. It was a natural for Reed, whose background was corporate marketing and management. Any profits generated from book sales go to the library.[14]

Another good example of a *win-win* intrapreneurial project was the provision of library services, for a contractual fee, to young educational institutions offered by Steely Library at Northern Kentucky University. Service agreements were negotiated between Steely Library and two customer institutions: a new community college, and a new branch campus of a for-profit institution. The resulting contracts allowed the institutions to immediately provide their faculty and student bodies with access to extensive information resources at very little cost. Use of Steely Library's established collections and document delivery and interlibrary loan services allowed the two customer institutions to start building their own library services on the public services side rather than investing in collections and technical services. When the two institutions were better established, they were able to more easily bring library support in-house. In the meantime, Steely Library had received substantial revenues through the contracts.

Always be sure that you can articulate the benefit accruing from any intrapreneurial effort, and most importantly, work to derive benefits for multiple constituencies, including the library, to those you are providing services to, and potentially to other third parties. A new service may provide users with better access to information, enrich the lives and experience of employees, and improve the standing and credibility of the library, opening up possibilities for continuing or increased support from the parent organization.

An example of this can also be found in Steely Library at Northern Kentucky University. The creation of a bachelor's degree program as well as a professional continuing education program in library science was an innovative, and perhaps counterintuitive, development within an academic library. However, it has provided benefits to a number of constituencies, including library staff from libraries throughout the country (professional education), library users served by graduates of the programs (stronger library services), Steely Library faculty (teaching opportunities, renewal of skills, added compensation), the library itself (revenue, improved librarian skills, opportunities for support-staff development, enhanced profile on campus), and the university (increased enrollment, revenue). In addition, the new programs have been leveraged as the basis of two major statewide grant-funded programs, each providing additional benefits to a wider audience. This is a true win-win situation.

Ultimately, intrapreneurs agree that their hard work, risk, and vision are worth the end result. The main point is to take action, finish the project, and make a difference. Change agents see opportunities where others see only obstacles. An idea may begin as a good intention, but if it is not developed and put into action with recognizable results, it remains only an idea. Management expert Peter Drucker noted that non-profit institutions, such as libraries, bring about change in people through services by creating "habits, vision, commitment, knowledge" and "become a part of the recipient rather than merely a supplier."[15]

As library professional and 2012–2013 Association of College & Research Libraries president Steven J. Bell observed, "librarians often fear success more than failure, as success means having to do the real work to make an idea come to fruition."[16] Author and entrepreneur Seth Godin echoed Bell's remarks and stated that the difference between success and failure comes after the idea is introduced. He asked, "Did you finish?"[17]

The ability to keep on track, focus on, and finish a project is a key component of the successful change agent. Innovation and intrapreneurship benefit all of those involved, from you, the intrapreneur, to your organization and its mission, your colleagues, your leaders, your community, and especially your clientele (see also Figure 2.3).

Self-confidence is an important factor in successfully becoming an intrapreneur. The greatest barrier to personal success is a lack of confidence in one's self. Everyone suffers from occasional self-doubts and anxieties. What will be the consequences of one's actions? The key is to overcome these doubts, anxieties, and fears by putting them into proper perspective. Begin by acknowledging your greatest self-doubt or fear. Is it

- failure and ridicule?
- public humiliation?
- covert backbiting, criticism, and sabotage?
- fear of making a mistake?
- blame?
- job termination?
- people saying that your idea is stupid?
- people saying that your concept is impossible?

An entrepreneurial spirit encouraged Zach Underwood, Julie Hart, and Nathan Lynn to provide digital access to the McCracken Kentucky County Public Library's unique special collection stored in the Local and Family History Department. Beginning with postcards, the  team worked with support from their administration and board of trustees to internally digitize and create metadata for the first collection. Receiving an expanded budget, the team was able to outsource more difficult items such as books, film reels, and negatives. Underwood noted: "We've added assistants and clerks to the project that are both interested in the material we're digitizing and knowledgeable about the history of Paducah. This has made metadata creation (by far the most time-consuming aspect of the process) much easier and more detailed and accurate." This unique digital collection is freely available online at http://digitalcollections.mclib.net, generates hundreds of visits monthly.

Figure 2.3: Swamp Roots[18]
Source: Photo courtesy of the McCracken County, Kentucky, Public Library Local and Family History Department, Mary Wheeler Collection. Features roustabout Uncle John at work. According to Underwood "Roustabouts were African-American river workers, and Mary Wheeler, of Paducah, was famous for collecting and transcribing their work songs. Uncle John is credited with the song 'Katie an' the Jim Lee Had a Little Race.'"

Or are you frightened of success? What if your project becomes a roaring success and you are suddenly propelled outside of your comfort zone? As entrepreneur Seth Godin writes, "success can be just as fraught with danger as failure, because it opens more doors and carries more responsibility."[19] Success means that you have to complete or develop the project, possibly replicate it, and continue to take risks and fight battles. It may also mean leaving your comfort zone and the confines of a familiar, if sometimes monotonous, work environment and heading into a more challenging and ever-changing role. Success also may mean stepping out into the community and engaging others in support of your idea. Success may mean more work. People say they want change, but are they really willing to implement it? How can intrapreneurs overcome fear?

Begin by addressing the fears and conquering them. Start with a sense of cold, hard reality. What is the worst thing that can happen? Address your excuses by listing and then countering them. Do not dwell on reasons for not beginning a project. Focus on the rewards for success rather than the consequences for failure. And above all, remember that your fears are not unique. All intrapreneurs have fears and doubts. The trick is to overcome them.

In spite of what may seem like negatives, success, with or without self-doubt and fear, remains one of the motivators intrapreneurs embrace in their quest to introduce innovative and policy- and organization-changing ideas. Intrapreneurs are self-starters and are more than capable of tapping into their own internal motivators.

The rewards of intrapreneurship can take many forms, including personal recognition, awards (such as those Movers and Shakers highlighted in *Library Journal*), more authority and responsibility, job flexibility, promotions, and, yes, additional compensation. However, the greatest reward for most intrapreneurs is the knowledge that their idea has been brought to life and that it benefits their organization, clientele, and community. Their efforts have made a difference.

Intrapreneurial Qualities

Intrapreneurs take action. . . . True intrapreneurs are trustworthy, encouraging, open, positive, supportive, and give credit where it's due!
—Howard E. Haller, Founder and Chief Enlightenment Officer of the Intrapreneurship Institute[20]

Our present system of management structure and decision distribution is safe and comfortable, but it doesn't work. . . . The discipline must come from within, because . . . nobody else cares what we do, only how much we spend. Many in our user communities, of course, would just as soon we changed nothing that is already comfortable. That is unacceptable, because it trivializes our own professional role.
—Herbert S. White[21]

The first commandment in Pinchot's original "The Intrapreneur's Ten Commandments," referring to corporate entrepreneurs, rather dauntingly reads: "Come to work each day willing to be fired." He amends this extreme directive a bit with additional commandments: "Don't ask to be fired; even as you bend the rules and act without permission, use all the political skill you and your sponsors can muster to move the project forward without making waves."[22] You want to become your organization's intrapreneur-in-residence, not an unemployed librarian. Indeed the authors of *Verbal Judo* caution: "the moment you stop thinking like your employer, you'd better start looking for another job."[23] Simply stated, put your organization first. It is not all about you. "Intrapreneurship isn't about grabbing the limelight, building an empire or using the company to catapult out but is more about turning an idea into an opportunity for the company."[24]

Pinchot further suggests that intrapreneurs "ask for advice before asking for resources," "express gratitude," and perhaps most importantly, "build your team; intrapreneuring is not a solo activity" as well as "share credit widely."[25] Indeed, just because you think you have the greatest idea since the online catalog does not mean that those you work for and with will be convinced. You are the one who is responsible for convincing others!

Part of the job of persuading others rests on your personal reputation within the organization and externally with your clientele. Personal trust and respect stem from working collegially with others, both within and outside of the organization, and advocating for your organization. Ask yourself some essential questions:

- How much do your colleagues and supervisors trust and respect you?
- Do you have a record of completing tasks on time?
- Are you pulling your weight in the organization?
- How do your clientele value you and your work?
- Do others perceive that you are a positive influence?
- Do you complete your work in a transparent environment and provide updates?
- Are you willing to share the credit for success and personally accept the repercussions of potential failure?
- Do you completely understand your organization, its goals, and its mission?
- Do you recognize your clientele and their needs?

How you handle conflict is a key component to success. Intrapreneurs who continue to push an idea out of sheer stubbornness without considering constructive criticism and revising the concept are usually not successful. Do not look at the intrapreneurial process as a *win-lose* scenario. If you have to modify, postpone, or terminate a project, this does not represent a loss for you personally. Rather, being able to adapt, being open to criticism and change, should be one of your primary objectives.

In addition to remaining open and responsive to your organization's needs, every intrapreneur's toolbox should contain the fine art of gracefully accepting "no." When intrapreneurs say "no" they oftentimes wonder what part of that statement is incomprehensible to others. When others say "no" to intrapreneurs, they question the decision and may frequently decide that they should never have to accept "no" for an answer. Taking that advice literally can place an intrapreneur in a very risky position.

First, learn to understand the nuanced meanings of "no." The organization's administration is charged to manage resources prudently, to set overall direction, and to coordinate the mission with that of a parent organization. The administration must also weigh proposals from throughout the organization to match them with the organization's ongoing mission and must balance between competing ideas. Not all ideas can be funded or supported at the same time, particularly if they (1) are contradictory, (2) require the same resources, (3) do not meet the organization's mission. If you decide to proceed without asking, and effectively convincing those people who have the power to reinforce "no," be prepared to be reprimanded, disciplined, or dismissed.

On the other hand, "no" can sometimes mean "not now." In that case, taking the time to better prepare your case, doing background work, proceeding with experiments—possibly on your own time—will enable you to better persuade management when the moment is ripe. Remember that effective intrapreneurship must welcome collaboration between an employer and an employee who both have the best interests of the organization in mind.

If you hear an unqualified "no" once too often you may feel that management is simply not open to new ideas, and it may be time to look for another job. Moving to an organization that encourages change from one that does not can pay big dividends in job satisfaction and reduced stress. Making an organizational move and also moving up the administrative ladder gives you a better platform to implement your idea.

By championing an idea intrapreneurs may encounter push-back and open themselves to a variety of risks. Ideas, especially organization-changing disruptive ones, may place the existing organization, clientele, operating policies, and power structures at risk. Unlike the entrepreneur, however, the intrapreneur does not endure personal *financial* risks, barring, of course, getting fired from his job! Intrapreneurs tap into the resources of their organizations and still receive a paycheck. When entrepreneurs fail, they may face personal bankruptcy as well as the loss of their idea and company. When intrapreneurs fail, the organization absorbs the costs of that failure. Nonetheless, intrapreneurs must be genuine risk takers. In many cases the amount of risk with which they feel comfortable will affect the degree to which they will succeed at intrapreneurship. Other factors influencing risk taking and its impacts include the organizational culture of your institution, which we will discuss more fully in Chapter 4.

Generally speaking, however, it is risk versus reward that characterizes a key difference between the psyche of intrapreneurs and entrepreneurs. Entrepreneurs elect to live in a risk-laden world that swings between huge rewards, usually monetary, on the one hand to enormous losses, also monetary, on the other. Intrapreneurs freely choose a steady paycheck within a stable and established organization with little expectation for large financial gains, although they may risk their own reputation within the organization. They work to achieve intrinsic gains rather than monetary rewards. While entrepreneurs sacrifice their time as well as their finances, intrapreneurs take risks with their own time as well as the organization's time—both precious commodities. In many ways, perhaps the most important sacrifice of all is time.

Once you acknowledge that your innovation is important assess the risks or potential costs to you personally. Are you comfortable risking something that you value highly, such as your standing in the organization or your free time, to see your idea implemented? If the answer is "yes" then it is time to assess what risks or costs most affect library intrapreneurs. As noted above, a major potential cost for many intrapreneurs is time, more specifically, the extra unpaid overtime you, the intrapreneur, will put into researching and defining the project while competently maintaining all duties as assigned. It also means taking the time to understand the big picture for your organization and how people, products, services, and internal and external influences interrelate. Bottom line: it means extra work!

Additional work and expending extra time are two key components of the risks and sacrifices an intrapreneur will accept to pursue her innovation. When the director of libraries at a major public university in the Southwest offered librarians the opportunity to learn new skills by paying for classes, many were reluctant to take up the offer. Why? It would cost their time, time in addition to their regular job duties. After all, those supporting the general consensus chanted: "we should be able to learn everything we need to learn during the work day." Others embraced the offer and donated their own time to attend classes, do homework, and learn new skills. When a manager who headed up one of the library's departments took up the challenge, she made the hour-long drive to a nearby community college for night classes to learn a new concept: online manipulation of images. Today, multiple apps and platforms make this an easily accessible skill, but in the late 1980s, this was not the case. Her new skills led to innovative work on physical touch screen kiosks in consultation with people inside and outside of the library. The result was that the library introduced a unique new product that predated the media-rich environment that we now experience through the Internet.[26]

So where does all this leave the budding intrapreneur or change agent? You already have a full plate. You are the dreamer, an innovator, the one who knows that change is needed, yet feels most comfortable working within your organization. You, as the library intrapreneur, desire change, but you are not quite sure if you want to put in the time to make it happen—not quite sure where to start. We'll go over many of the details, but remember that Pinchot characterized intrapreneurs as the "dreamers who do." Intrapreneurs dream and collaborate with others to make their dream a reality.[27] Figure 2.4 illustrates the characteristics of successful change agents.

Intrapreneurs and change agents are not that arrogant and overbearing colleague with a plan that is better than anyone else could ever construct. They are not the incarnation of that glamorous, successful, and rather fictitious, billionaire entrepreneur who runs roughshod over everyone and everything in pursuit of a single goal. While you can certainly stretch the imagination, push the envelope, and think outside the box, never forget that everyone has the ability to be creative, and without support in an organization your innovation may face an early demise. Instead of stepping on toes and bruising heads, why not inspire others to join you in bringing your innovation to light? If you are an intrapreneurial manager, the greatest triumph is to build buy-in from your employees. Encourage them to take your idea and develop it as their own. What you gain in quality and satisfaction will more than compensate you for lack of credit or loss of control over your idea. They may even make it better. Figure 2.5 illustrates the negative characteristics that could derail any change agent.

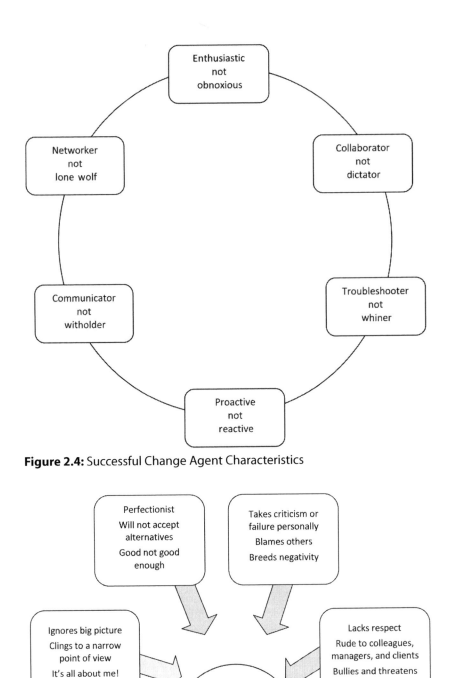

Figure 2.4: Successful Change Agent Characteristics

Figure 2.5: What Change Agents Are Not

How to Measure Success

Talent that cannot be shared, duplicated, distributed, or leveraged is not nearly as valuable as talent that can.

Mike Myatt[28]

Success for a library is always defined in terms of the community served. . . . A library cannot be successful apart from its community.

Andrea D. Berstler[29]

Virgin Group founder Richard Branson remarks, "My definition of success? The more you're actively and practically engaged, the more successful you will feel."[30] Being engaged with your job and your talents are key components not only to success, but to personal and professional contentment, but how do you measure *success*?

That said stress and conflict are a part of an intrapreneur's existence. Intrapreneurs must work within competitive systems to create, sell, and market their products or services. Seth Godin, author and entrepreneur, promotes the concept that through your own efforts, passion, and commitment you can become a linchpin rather than a cog in your workplace. Even these two terms hark back to the industrial age. A cog in the machine is a part of a gear or wheel that is turned by other forces; the linchpin holds the cogs together.[31] Good advice for the budding change agent: be the best you can be, but remember that no one is indispensable and even if you are the most innovative person in the world, if you abuse your position, people will not want to work with you to achieve your goals.

Mike Myatt, leadership advisor to Fortune 500 CEOs and boards, comments that nobody "and I mean nobody is indispensable. I don't care who you are, what role you play, or what your title is—if you perceive yourself to be indispensable, you are setting yourself up for a very rude awakening. I was once reminded that the graveyards are full of indispensable people."[32]

No one need be satisfied with being a cog in the machine. This begs the question whether managers can also be intrapreneurial? The answer is an emphatic "yes." Those with vision outside of the conventional mold create the intrapreneurial culture within an organization that is crucial to innovation.

Intrapreneur Questions

No matter what your status is in your organization, no matter how big or small your library, no matter how many are on staff, no matter what type of library or organization you work in, no matter how dismal the

Questions to Consider	Answers—Give Details
List the reasons and fears that may be keeping you from moving forward with your innovation idea?	
What idea do you have for a new or enhanced product or service that your organization can provide? Can you articulate your idea? (More about the elevator speech and selling your ideas in Chapter 6.)	
On a scale of 1 to 5, with 1 being not very enthusiastic and 5 being exceedingly enthusiastic, rate how enthusiastic you are about this idea.	1 2 3 4 5
Can you see the big picture for your organization? Why or why not is this important?	
Is your innovation idea internal or external to your library? Or both?	
What partnerships do you see within and outside of your library that can enhance your library's ability to serve its clientele both in the library and through distributed services?	
Have you ever presented an idea to your boss at an inappropriate time and been shot down in flames so that you never wanted to suggest anything again? Did you keep thinking and wondering if you could have presented the idea in a better way? At a better time? If so, you need to consider both an elevator speech, feasibility study, and an idea implementation plan—also known as an innovator's plan—see Chapter 6. The innovator's plan is in chapter 6.	
Do you work effectively and collegially with your supervisors and peers? Name an example.	
Do you practice optimism? Is your glass half full or half empty? Are you usually positive or negative? are you always negative? Give examples.	
Are you averse to taking any risks, but want to effect substantial change in your organization? Why or why not? Define risk as you see it within your organization.	
How much time are you willing to commit to a project? Can you negotiate time commitments in your position?	

Figure 2.6: Intrapreneur Questions

Do you take the time to think through ideas and present them to colleagues? How do you do this?	
Have you invested your time to make sure you have all your "ducks in a row," or did you simply sound off in a meeting hoping someone else would do all the work? Do you have the tenacity to invest your time and efforts to make a plan and convince others that you can make your idea a reality?	
Have you wondered how to become a change agent for your library, but don't know whom to approach? Have you tried talking with your colleagues, your supervisor, the board of directors, the director/dean?	
How do you convince your boss(es) to let you try a new idea even if all you hear is that you cannot waste resources or make a mistake! Consider how you can present a comprehensive plan with goals and financial forecasting.	

Figure 2.6: (continued)

budget, you can become an entrepreneur-in-residence, an intrapreneur, a change agent, a linchpin rather than a cog. Invest time in yourself, your innovation, and your organization. Let's start with a number of general questions that you need to ask yourself as you assess your abilities and commitment. Use Figure 2.6 to answer these questions. You may answer "yes" or "no," but be sure to explain why you did.

Based on your answers in the questionnaire, are you invigorated and inspired? Hopefully, you are more energized and anxious to consider your next steps for success. Keep focused and don't allow outside influences or a crisis or catastrophe to be the only source of change in your organization. Focus on what you, the intrapreneur, can do to make a difference in your organization. In Chapter 3, we will look at some ways to focus and enhance your creative genius and help you to become the change agent that truly makes a difference.

Notes

1. Douglas S. Brown, "Unhappy at Work? Be an Intrapreneur." *Community Content*, May 13, 2013, http://www.wired.com/2013/05/unhappy-at-work-be-an-intrapreneur/. Post University is in Waterbury, Connecticut.

2. Gifford Pinchot, III, and Elizabeth S. Pinchot, "Intra-Corporate Entrepreneurship," Intrapreneur.com, Fall 1978, http://www.intrapreneur.com/MainPages/History/IntraCorp.html. Pinchot cofounded the Bainbridge Graduate Institute in 2002, which was renamed Pinchot University in 2015. Their mission was and is to "change business for good." They offer certificates and MBAs in sustainable business along with the Center for Inclusive Entrepreneurship program. For more information, visit the school's Web site: http://pinchot.edu/.

3. Gerald C. Lubenow, "Jobs Talks about His Rise and Fall," *Newsweek*, September 29, 1985, http://www.newsweek.com/jobs-talks-about-his-rise-and-fall-207016.

4. Kevin C. DeSouza, *Intrapreneurship: Managing Ideas within Your Organization* (Toronto: University of Toronto Press, 2011), 5.

5. Ibid., 34.

6. Donald F. Kuratko and Richard M. Hodgetts, *Entrepreneurship: Theory, Process, Practice*, 7th ed. (Mason, OH: Thomson Higher Education, 2007), 55.

7. Guy Kawasaki, *The Art of the Start: The Time-Tested, Battle-Hardened Guide for Anyone Starting Anything* (New York: Penguin, 2004), 20.

8. Dan Schawbel discussed the importance of intrapreneurship for millennials as "an opportunity to develop their leadership skills while inspiring change. For millennials who are entrepreneurial, but are still paying back student loans and don't have access to mentors or capital, intrapreneurship is the perfect solution. By leveraging internal resources and a corporate brand, millennials can make a big impact even at the start of their careers—and that's exactly what they want. When intrapreneurs are successful, companies reap the benefits too." Dan Schawbel, "Why Companies Want You to Become an Intrapreneur," *Forbes*, September 9, 2013, http://www.forbes.com/sites/danschawbel/2013/09/09/why-companies-want-you-to-become-an-intrapreneur/.

9. Entrelib: The Conference for Entrepreneurial Librarians, http://entrelib.org/.

10. Matthew G. Kenney, *Academic Entrepreneurship: The Role of Intrapreneurship in Developing Faculty Job Satisfaction* (Saarbrücken: VDM, 2009), 2–3.

11. Lisa Peet, "Academic Movers 2015: In Depth with Kyle Courtney," *Library Journal*, June 4, 2015, http://lj.libraryjournal.com/2015/06/people/academic-movers/academic-movers-2015-in-depth-with-kyle-courtney/.

12. Diamond Law Library, "Fee Based Services," Columbia University, c. 2016, http://web.law.columbia.edu/library/services/fee-based.

13. Elizabeth A. McDaniel and Ronald H. Epp, "Fee-Based Information Services: The Promises and Pitfalls of a New Revenue Source in Higher Education," *CAUSE/EFFECT* (Summer 1995), 35–39.

14. "Up with Upcycling," Mindy Reed, Movers & Shakers 2015—Innovators, *Library Journal*, March 17, 2015, http://lj.libraryjournal.com/2015/03/people/movers-shakers-2015/mindy-reed-movers-shakers-2015-innovators/.

15. Peter Drucker, *Managing the Non-Profit Organization: Practices and Principles* (New York: Harper Collins, 1990), 39.

16. Steven J. Bell, "The Librarian Entrepreneur? Demystifying an Oxymoron," *Against the Grain* 21, no. 4 (2009), 20. Check Bell's Web site: http://blended librarian.learningtimes.net/.

17. Seth Godin, *Linchpin: Are You Indispensable?* (New York: Portfolio, 2010), 136.

18. Zach Underwood, e-mail messages to authors, June 23, 2015, and July 1, 2015.

19. Seth Godin, *The Icarus Deception: How High Will You Fly?* (New York: Portfolio/Penguin, 2012), 183.

20. Howard Edward Haller, *Intrapreneurship. The Secret to: Ignite Innovation, Recruit and Retain Key Employees, Unlock New Product Creation, Expand Market Share, Sustain Higher Profits, Improve Job Satisfaction* (Coeur d'Alene, Idaho: Silver Eagle, 2014), 32–3. Check Haller's Web site: http://www.intrapreneurshipinstitute.com/.

21. Herbert S. White, "Entrepreneurship and the Library Profession," *Journal of Library Administration* 8, no. 1 (Spring 1987): 27.

22. Gifford Pinchot, III, "The Intrapreneur's Ten Commandments," *The Pinchot Perspective*, November 20, 2011, http://www.pinchot.com/perspective/intrapreneuring/.

23. George J. Thompson and Jerry B. Jenkins, *Verbal Judo: The Gentle Art of Persuasion* (New York: William Morrow, 2013), 54.

24. Anastasia, "Intrapreneur," *Entrepreneurial Insights*, March 25, 2015, http://www.entrepreneurial-insights.com/lexicon/intrapreneur/.

25. Gifford Pinchot, "The Intrapreneur's Ten Commandments," *The Pinchot Perspective*, November 20, 2011, http://www.pinchot.com/2011/11/the-intrapreneurs-ten-commandments.html.

26. Sharon Almquist, Head, Media Library, University of North Texas Libraries, took classes at Collin County Community College and Richland College.

27. Gifford Pinchot, "Innovation through Intrapreneuring," *Research Management* 20, no. 2 (March-April 1987), http://www.intrapreneur.com/MainPages/History/InnovThruIntra.html.

28. Mike Myatt, "Seth Godin's Linchpin Theory: Sound Advice or Career Suicide?," *Forbes*, November 29, 2011. Leadership, http://www.forbes.com/sites/mikemyatt/2011/11/29/seth-godins-linchpin-theory-sound-advice-or-career-suicide/.

29. Andrea D. Berstler, "Running the Library as a Business," in *The Entrepreneurial Librarian: Essays on the Infusion of Private-Business Dynamism into Professional Service*, Mary Krautter, Mary Beth Lock, and Mary G. Scanlon, eds. (Jefferson, NC: McFarland, 2012), 30.

30. Richard Branson, "My Definition of Success," *Virgin*, http://www.virgin.com/richard-branson/my-definition-of-success.

31. Godin, *Linchpin: Are You Indispensable?*, 136.

32. Myatt, "Seth Godin's Linchpin Theory."

CHAPTER 3

Agent of Change and the Art of Intrapreneurial Innovation

There is nothing more difficult and dangerous, or more doubtful of success, than an attempt to introduce a new order of things.
— Niccolò Machiavelli, *The Prince*[1]

Machiavelli's ageless quote illustrates the perils facing any change agent at any time. Passionate intrapreneurs are change agents who identify a need for improvement and work to create opportunities, products, or services. They embrace change because they want to create something better: a product, a service, a social condition. Change agents are committed and adaptable enough to create sustainable and enriching change through proactive insight, knowledge, networking, and interaction with their colleagues.

Several 21st-century authors reflected on Machiavelli's 16th-century statement illustrating how, in attempting to persuade others to invest in an idea, change agents virtually guaranteed disagreement: "The more intensely you live, the more you choose to make a difference in the world, the more you create vital, as opposed to insipid, relationships, then the more open you are to whacks and bumps and bruises. That's the only path to honest, bottom-line communication."[2]

An effective way to recognize and communicate intrapreneurial library efforts is through reading the literature. One specific outlet is the *Library Journal* (*LJ*)'s annual Movers and Shakers awards. *LJ* has acknowledged library change agents and innovators since 2002 with these various awards, which highlight those individuals, librarians, and others who work in libraries, information centers, or vendor businesses, and have made meaningful change within their organizations, resulting in new or improved services. They serve as models for others to emulate as well as a way to present distinctive ideas and solutions worth copying. As *LJ* editor-in-chief Francine Fialkoff noted, "We wanted to reach down below the directors, the heads of departments, corporations, or institutions, to identify up-and-comers in all areas of librarianship, whether they are working in libraries or not."[3] Increasing from 51 recommendations in 2002 to over 300 in 2015, *LJ* Movers and Shakers are people who are passionate about libraries, embrace innovative thinking, and turn their ideas into realities. Between 2002 and 2015, over 700 people have received the award.

LJ uses a variety of categories to illustrate impact, in such areas as technical, social, and educational intrapreneurship, and includes people working in libraries at all levels. Consider where you fit in, but be aware that categories overlap as services and products change to reflect the transformative process that is so crucial to library intrapreneurship. *LJ* recognizes the following categories:

- Community builders: Those dreamers who deliver new library services vital to a community "whether by creating an entirely new place to gather online or reinventing a rundown library as a neighborhood hub."[4]

- Visionaries: Change agents who lead through their ideas and are not bound or burdened by past "mistakes." Some have even learned a great deal from "failures." Sometimes today's mistakes are tomorrow's innovations.

- Mentors: Experienced professionals who invest their time to share knowledge and assist new generations in the field of librarianship. Frequently, innovators working with an experienced librarian outside of their organization can collaborate and share ideas and innovations.

- Activists: Those for whom librarianship is not only a passion, but a place to extend ideas to successfully enhance service to others. "If information and knowledge unlock power, these professionals see it as their duty to make sure everyone has access to the keys."[5] Librarians have always advocated for accessible information for everyone.

- Innovators: These individuals, from all walks of librarianship, including vendors, recognize problems and take action to provide solutions for better, and frequently unique, services or products.[6] They dream, unfettered by budget constraints.

- Collection developers: These individuals focus on increasing the scope and quality of materials that may be accessed through libraries, going beyond collections owned by the library itself.[7] What constitutes a collection has greatly changed over the years. In 2002, the basis for this award acknowledged continual change, but noted that "collections remain the foundation of our increasingly diverse institutions."[8]

- Scholars: Librarians, both generalists and specialists, who strive to find new ideas and open the doors for new ways of learning. Many librarians enjoy learning new things and expanding their knowledge. They "dig deep and apply focused knowledge to benefit users and fellow librarians."[9]

- Team players: Individuals who embrace and live the team concept. No one, especially the successful intrapreneur, works in a vacuum.

- Service providers: While all individuals in libraries provide some sort of service, this award recognizes innovators who consider that "each encounter is a unique opportunity to help, as well as a source of inspiration for new ways to reach users."[10]

- Change agents: A general term *LJ* uses for people in libraries who are successful innovators and implementers within their organizations (see Figure 3.1 for an example of an *LJ* change agent in action).

- Educators: From creating college credit-bearing and non-credit continuing education programs to using digital techniques to make materials more accessible, educators have changed lives in innovative ways and *LJ* acknowledges these contributions.

- Digital developers, or technology leaders: *LJ* highlights those people who stand on the cutting edge in using emerging technologies in innovative ways in librarianship.

- Marketers: *LJ* has changed this category throughout the years to include those adept at marketing or branding, thereby making their libraries more visible to the community.

Elizabeth Joseph, Coordinator, Information & Adult Services, Ferguson Library, Stamford, Connecticut, took action when her city was hit with an economic downturn. Residents turned to the library for information, and Joseph saw how the library could help by creating an active partnership with local businesses and SCORE (Service Corps of Retired Executives), the nonprofit small business education organization. Together they created the Stamford Small Business Resource Center, which opened in the main library in November 2013. "[Elizabeth] has the unique ability to take a deficit or challenge and turn it into an opportunity," says Ferguson Library president Alice Knapp. "She doesn't let problems such as staffing or funding get in the way of providing superior library service." Key points for all change agents to remember.

Figure 3.1: Change Agents in Action[11]

LJ provides a set of resources and tools for keeping abreast of innovations and changes in librarianship called Lead the Change (LTC) and the LTC Leadership Academy—Online. This series of live events and webcasts serves as a great area for innovators to come together, learn, and discuss their ideas. The LTC Commons offers an online community where "library professionals can share resources, make connections, and crowdsource solutions to their challenges."[12]

Creativity, Communication, Collaboration

Like electricity, creativity makes no judgment. I can use it productively or destructively. The important thing is to use it. You can't use up creativity. The more you use it, the more you have.

—Maya Angelou[13]

Creativity is a somewhat mysterious, yet inspired, process that allows people to think, reason, and envision outcomes beyond obvious practicalities, often while constructing unique combinations and connections between people, organizations, and resources. It means seeing relationships where others see chaos, identifying patterns, envisioning partnerships and relationships between previously unrelated people, services, and ideas. Creativity refers to the ability to effectively generate novel solutions to pertinent problems or generate new ideas out of current concerns.

Creativity often appears as the first stage in the innovation process and flourishes as possibilities, probabilities, and opportunities are combined to overcome perceived and real challenges. It requires the intrapreneurial change agent to approach the process with a positive attitude. Creativity is energetic; it focuses on viewing your job and the world through a different window. It is an invitation to think differently; to perceive common issues through a new lens. It allows you to keep pace with constant environmental change.

Creativity is a process that inspires individuals to find new solutions that may be useful and appropriate to your organization. However, while you brainstorm for *pie in the sky* ideas, remember change for change's sake is not the desired end result—in fact it may be a problem! That is, creativity should lead to effective innovations, ranging from minor changes or improvements critical to your organization's mission, to radical change, such as new services or organizational divisions. Effective applications of creativity can enhance any organizational task, including departmental work flows, management decisions, marketing, or problem solving.

Creativity is both an art and a process, as the English psychologist Graham Wallas discussed in his 1926 study of creativity titled *The Art of Thought*. Wallas, one of the first to research and develop a description of the creative process, suggested four stages:

1. Preparation: You consciously explore an opportunity or problem in multiple ways through research and planning. You basically plunge yourself into the issue. You read and discuss and understand what others might be doing with a similar issue.

2. Incubation: You do not consciously think about an opportunity or problem; you set it aside and let it simmer in the background.

3. Illumination: You see solutions and different associations. Wallas noted: "Sometimes the successful train seems to consist of a single leap of association, or of successive leaps which are so rapid as to be almost instantaneous."[14]

4. Verification: You consciously test and evaluate.

Wallas's model allows innovators to evaluate where they are in the innovation process. As with other idea generators, the four steps in Wallas's process are interrelated and allow you to examine ideas and solutions in different ways. Such processes certainly tie in with Gifford Pinchot's discussion of the types of questions intrapreneurs should ask: "Who would I need to help me with this? How much would it cost? What things have to happen first?"[15]

Creativity may appear as an individual inspiration, but collaboration and communication are required to get the job done. Invite others to look through that new window with you. Successful intrapreneurial change agents do not work alone; they coordinate with others. Change agents who received *LJ* Movers and Shakers awards in 2014 collectively noted: "that they couldn't succeed without their colleagues, so, in effect, the Movers & Shakers represent hundreds more who work in and for libraries."[16] Collegial collaboration is the key to successful creativity solutions and innovation within an organization.

It is important to remember that innovation in itself, like change for change's sake, is not a solution; it is a multistep process that starts with your ability to see a need or opportunity and then use your skills in communication and collaboration to formulate a solution. Creativity can encourage successful innovations or improvements. This is crucial because oftentimes innovation in a public service organization is defeated by its own self-imposed impediments, missions, and attitudes. Realize that you will encounter resistance, but persevere. Don't step on toes; invite anti-change agents to dance with you instead. Consider an idea a prime opportunity to do something differently or to design an entirely new service. Avoid viewing resistance as a threat. Consider it your opportunity to communicate effectively why a change is needed and explain how the outcome is beneficial to the organization. Intrapreneurial success depends on communication: effective communication with others within your organization as well as with external clientele.

A lack of communication is often blamed for project failures. The difficulties of communication may be illustrated with this oft-repeated quote: "The single biggest problem in communication is the illusion that it has been accomplished."[17] Effective change agents are also effective communicators. Why? Because they have learned to listen and empathize with those with whom they wish to communicate. They do not make assumptions.

Intrapreneurship and Strategy

Just as entrepreneurs are governed by their corporation's bylaws and are accountable to a board of directors, intrapreneurs are governed by the goals of their library and parent organization and are accountable to the organization's administration. If you wonder whether your idea will fit the purpose of your organization, do your homework. Begin by reading and understanding your library's strategic-planning documents, particularly the mission and vision statements. If your library or parent organization lacks these documents, it is probably time for the organization's administration to formulate them. This is a part of the strategic-planning process that asks probing questions about the current and future direction of the organization and lists organizational goals and steps for their accomplishment. While a complete discussion of strategic planning is beyond the scope of this book, a few words of advice may be helpful.

It is important to remember that the purpose of the process is the creation of a strategy, not the creation of a plan. Many organizations get so involved in the planning process that they produce an impressive plan but forget to strategize. The result is a plan that is read, filed, and forgotten, or one that is so rigid that it inhibits innovation at all levels.

Keep your organization's efforts focused on activities related to its purpose. In the library setting, that does not mean focusing only on traditional library services and functions, but it does mean keeping the focus on products and services that make best use of the unique skills, perspectives, and resources that we bring to the table as librarians.

On the other hand, be open to new opportunities and willing to project the unique attributes of libraries to provide solutions for their users and parent organizations. Look for opportunities that benefit multiple constituencies, such as the example that appeared in Chapter 2, the bachelor and continuing education programs started by Steely Library at NKU. In that example the library, the university, the profession, and the greater public all benefited from the creation of these programs.

A part of the planning process may include the traditional strengths, weaknesses, opportunities, threats (SWOT) method. SWOT encourages all participants to think and take stock of the environment, considering and balancing the organization's strengths and opportunities against its weaknesses and threats.

As part of the planning process, the mission and vision statements are key components. Try to keep mission and vision statements short and to the point—tweetable, if possible. This also opens possibilities for publicizing the statements in many ways: banners, signage, printed promotional materials as well as through social media.

Examine your library's mission and vision statements and evaluate their effectiveness. Below are examples of effective statements.

1. Daniel Boone Regional Library, Boone and Calloway Counties and Columbia, Missouri

   Mission: "DBRL connects our communities to the world of information and ideas."

   Vision: "DBRL's vision is to encourage reading and lifelong learning. Everyone in our diverse communities will have open access to library services that expand minds, empower individuals and enrich lives."[18]

2. Michael Schwartz Library, Cleveland State University, Cleveland, Ohio

   Mission: "We bring people and information together."

   Vision: "The Library will be recognized as an accessible and exceptional center of research, learning, and creativity focused on student success. We will provide the best of contemporary and traditional research tools, unique local resources, and state of the art facilities to the CSU community and work to ensure that all its members are proficient information users. We will be leaders in developing and utilizing the talents of everyone who works in the library to achieve excellence in service to students and to our community."[19]

3. Oak Park, Illinois, Public Library

   Mission: "The Oak Park Public Library enhances the quality of life in our diverse community by providing opportunities for lifelong learning, by creating spaces and opportunities to connect and engage, and by fostering a love of reading and commitment to literacy."

   Vision: "The Oak Park Public Library creates opportunities to participate, connect, and discover."[20]

4. Steely Library, Northern Kentucky University

   Mission: "Transforming people through information."

   Vision: "By focusing on our skills and perspectives, Steely Library will gain recognition for the unique value we provide in preparing individuals to succeed in a global information society."[21]

Be sure to fully examine your organization's vision and mission statements before jumping into the change arena. As noted before, change just to change or to champion your way of thinking without considering the vision and goals of the overall organization is neither sustainable nor effective.

Conflict

The rejectionists
We can choose to define ourselves (our smarts, our brand, our character) on who rejects us.
Or we can choose to focus on those that care enough to think we matter.
Carrying around a list of everyone who thinks you're not good enough is exhausting.

—Seth Godin[22]

It is true that worry about what others' think about you personally or your ideas is stressful and tiring. That is why effective change agents soothe reasonable conflict through collaboration. Change agents, whether internal or external, must be focused enough to neither create nor empower negative energy. They must work within the confines of an organization to create positive results.

Unfortunately, conflict frequently arises when your personal goals do not match those of others in your organization. Conflict may also arise when your goals do not align with those of your organization or administration. While you may be empowered, you are still accountable and in the end should be working to advance the mission of your organization, not simply to advance your own ends. The ability to creatively compromise is crucial. As noted before, change agents are not bull headed. Just as in other issues concerning the library, your initiatives must tie into the organization's overall plan, reflect its common goals, and be measurable. You must be able to articulate the benefits of your innovation.

That said there are, as shown in Figure 3.2, "reasons for not innovating or improving," many excuses we create to discourage ourselves from innovating or spearheading a change or from supporting another colleague's attempt at innovation.

Sounds familiar? Add to these negative impulses the annihilating factors of groupthink and the Abilene paradox.

Groupthink and the Abilene Paradox: Collective Dysfunction

In 1972 social psychologist Irving Janis created a term *groupthink* to describe the oftentimes horrendous results of dysfunctional group decisions. These occur when group pressures are allowed to override, intimidate, dehumanize, or otherwise ignore individuals. It is one thing to present an idea openly and ask for group support. It is quite another to have a dysfunctional team, which may not even know it is dysfunctional, make decisions for you. As we will discuss later in forming your team, many groups succumb to groupthink because their members are too similar or homogeneous and the group is allowed to function without seeking or accepting outside opinions. In addition, without a clear charge to support a

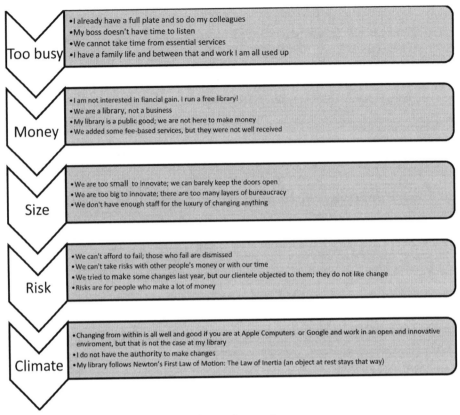

Too busy
- I already have a full plate and so do my colleagues
- My boss doesn't have time to listen
- We cannot take time from essential services
- I have a family life and between that and work I am all used up

Money
- I am not interested in fiancial gain. I run a free library!
- We are a library, not a business
- My library is a public good; we are not here to make money
- We added some fee-based services, but they were not well received

Size
- We are too small to innovate; we can barely keep the doors open
- We are too big to innovate; there are too many layers of bureaucracy
- We don't have enough staff for the luxury of changing anything

Risk
- We can't afford to fail; those who fail are dismissed
- We can't take risks with other people's money or with our time
- We tried to make some changes last year, but our clientele objected to them; they do not like change
- Risks are for people who make a lot of money

Climate
- Changing from within is all well and good if you are at Apple Computers or Google and work in an open and innovative enviroment, but that is not the case at my library
- I do not have the authority to make changes
- My library follows Newton's First Law of Motion: The Law of Inertia (an object at rest stays that way)

Figure 3.2: Reasons for Not Innovating or Improving

decision, the group is quite capable of going rogue and trampling individual initiative.

One prominent historical example of groupthink's often horrific results is the Bay of Pigs disaster in Cuba during the Kennedy administration, which Janis characterizes as "among the worst fiascoes ever perpetrated by a responsible government" even though those who planned it included some of the "most intelligent men ever to participate in the councils of government."[23] Of course, while library change agents need to avoid participating in or encouraging groupthink, their end results may not be on the same level as the fiascoes Janis analyzes. Be aware that if you make a conscious decision to defer to others' decisions through fear or boredom, or because they are your friends, you have participated in a form of groupthink. What is insidious about groupthink is that the members often feel good about their decisions.

Victims of the Abilene paradox, on the other hand, do not feel good about their decisions. Both processes are based on decisions that reflect attitudes geared more toward achieving a perceived consensus rather than effective communication. In the Abilene paradox a group of people consciously decide to do something that no one in the group really wants to do. Such agreement generally results in a bad decision. Jerry B. Harvey introduced the term in 1974, based on both the process and the title on a story, which goes something like this.

It is a hot Sunday summer afternoon in Coleman, Texas, just bearable if you sit still in front of a fan. Dust blows on the hot wind. Suddenly, one of the family suggests taking a trip into Abilene to eat dinner at the cafeteria. You all say "OK" without much conviction. Returning home after a heavy meal and an uncomfortable round trip of four hours in a non-air-conditioned car, you comment on what a great trip you just had. No one agrees. Everyone begins to blame each other for the decision and finally everyone realizes that no one really wanted to go in the first place. The group was unable to manage agreement, let alone disagreement, hence the paradox and the absurdity of the group's decision. The Abilene paradox is a prime example of unintentional and mismanaged agreement and misdirected communication.[24]

Innovations versus Improvements

So far we have defined *entrepreneur*, *intrapreneur*, and *change agent*, but what about *innovation*? It is a word we all use, and misuse frequently. What does it really mean, and does it have different nuances depending on who uses it? As the *Wall Street Journal* laments, "like the once ubiquitous buzzwords 'synergy' and 'optimization,' innovation is in danger of becoming a cliché—if it isn't one already."[25] Let's examine this much-used and abused term to ensure that change agents use it effactually and understand its ramifications.

- Entrepreneurial innovation: As discussed in Chapter 1, this refers to an independent individual or a group of individuals who create a novel idea or invention and render it into a product or service which people will pay for. The product or service must be reproducible at a reasonable cost and fulfill an explicitly acknowledged need. As noted in Chapter 1, Joseph Schumpeter called this process creative destruction, which occurred when new goods or services replaced those already existing.

Entrepreneurial innovation involves risk because a new product or service may fail to attract enough users to remain viable in its intended market. Innovative entrepreneurs take great risks and "live the Innovator's DNA." They question everything and observe "the world like anthropologists." They network and experiment in an effort to "figure out novel solutions, and connecting the typically unconnected insights to create disruptive new business ideas."[26] Consider how many of these bleeding edge ventures fail and how many succeed. Creating a novel, new, disruptive, transformative, world-changing, unique, totally different, problem-solving, innovative product or service involves a great deal of uncertainty, chaos, and risk. "Producing the next product (like the iPod) or creating a new market (Instagram, without a big team) that had never existed before—that is innovation."[27]

- Intrapreneurial innovation: Teams and individuals within an organization may incorporate elements of entrepreneurial innovation and produce an entirely new service or they may focus on major improvements to existing services and processes. Like many small businesses, most libraries are imitative in their products or services. A pizzeria is a pizzeria is a pizzeria, and a library is a library is a library. Both pizzeria and library provide the same basic services and functionality to their particular client base. To survive and thrive in a crowded environment, however, small business entrepreneurs seek to differentiate their product through innovative initiatives. Libraries should do the same thing. Intrapreneurial innovation should focus on projecting the unique strengths and resources specific to a library and emphasize the ways a library provides added value. Always be conscious of serving, growing, and diversifying the user base.

The other side of innovation is to streamline internal procedures. Innovating by extending or modifying existing services is equally important. For example, libraries may provide temporary boutique-type services that cater to a micro niche on a case-by-case basis. Pop-up libraries or onsite services could be another way in which to leverage and improve existing services to better address needs and improve usage.

Intrapreneurial change agents may spearhead permanent change, incremental improvements, or radical innovations within their organizations. They work with and through their organizations to offer solutions and meet unmet internal- and external-client needs. They donate their time, knowledge, and passion to provide effective service.

How to Be an Intrapreneur/ Change Agent/Innovator

> Intrapreneurship works only if people believe in themselves and their potential to make a contribution that goes beyond the performance of day-to-day tasks.
>
> —Kevin C. DeSouza[28]

> Certainly the nature of work is changing, and the highest value employees are those who can handle ambiguity and synthesizing enormous amounts of information into strategically useful tactics.
>
> —Chris Messina, agent of free will[29]

How can you determine if you have what it takes to be an intrapreneur/ change agent/innovator? You feel passionate about useful change and offering sustainable solutions. You have great ideas and want to implement them, but suffer from doubts. You fear failure, but are willing to take calculated risks to make meaningful change.

Change can be disruptive, but the opposite of change is stasis. As consultant Alan Cohen wrote, "it takes a lot of courage to release the familiar and seemingly secure, to embrace the new. But there is no real security in what is no longer meaningful. There is more security in the adventurous and exciting, for in movement there is life, and in change there is power."[30]

As we examine what constitutes a *good* idea in later chapters, remember the old adage: "as one man's meat is another man's poison, so one man's rubbish is another man's treasure."[31] Of course, the adage refers to the many different forms of garbage and their many and varied uses in 1879. In other words, don't be discouraged.

To help formulate your thoughts and hopefully avoid discouragement, use the Intrapreneur Test in Appendix A to help you analyze your skills. Consider each question carefully and truthfully answer it. When you are finished, look over some interpretations and comments in Appendix B. Chances are you are the change agent just waiting for the right time to innovate, to change, and to solve problems in your organization. Remember, it is acceptable to have doubts and to be concerned about risks. Innovation never happens without doubts and fears. Focus on the beneficial results of your ideas and remain passionate about your goals.

Notes

1. Niccolò Machiavelli, *The Historical, Political, and Diplomatic Writings of Niccolo Machiavelli*, trans. Christian E. Detmold (Boston: James R. Osgood, 1882) 20, https://books.google.com/books?id=pIFoAAAAMAAJ& pg=PP1#v=onepage&q&f=false. Other pertinent observations follow Machiavelli's initial statement: "The innovator has for enemies all those who derived advantages from the old order of things, whilst those who expect to be benefited by the new institutions will be but lukewarm defenders. . . . Whenever the opponents of the new order of things have the opportunity to attack it, they will do it with the zeal of partisans, whilst the others defend it but feebly, so that it is dangerous to rely upon the latter."
2. George J. Thompson and Jerry B. Jenkins, *Verbal Judo: The Gentle Art of Persuasion* (New York: William Morrow, 2013), 25.
3. Francine Fialkoff, ed., "Introduction, Change Agents," 2002 Movers & Shakers: The People Who Are Shaping the Future of Libraries. *Library Journal* 127, no. 5 (March 15, 2002), 6. Supplement.
4. "Visionaries," 2002 Movers & Shakers, 11.
5. "Activists," 2002 Movers & Shakers, 35.
6. "Innovators," 2002 Movers & Shakers, 43.
7. "Collection Developers," Movers & Shakers 2002, 51.
8. Ibid.
9. "Scholars," Movers & Shakers 2002, 57.
10. "Service Providers," Movers & Shakers 2002, 73.
11. Elizabeth Joseph, "Calling All Entrepreneurs," Movers & Shakers 2015, Innovators, *Library Journal*, March 17, 2015, http://lj.libraryjournal.com/2015/03/people/movers-shakers-2015/elizabeth-joseph-movers-shakers-2015-innovators/. Joseph received a *Library Journal* Movers and Shakers Award for Innovators in 2015.
12. "Lead the Change: Professional Development for Today's Librarian," *Library Journal*, http://lj.libraryjournal.com/lead-the-change/.
13. Jeffrey M. Elliot, ed., *Conversations with Maya Angelou* (Jackson: University Press of Mississippi, 1989), x.
14. Maria Popova, "The Art of Thought: Graham Wallas on the Four Stages of Creativity, 1926," *Brain Pickings*, http://www.brainpickings.org/2013/08/28/the-art-of-thought-graham-wallas-stages/.
15. Gifford Pinchot, "Innovation through Intrapreneuring," *Research Management* (March–April 1987), 20, 2, http://www.intrapreneur.com/MainPages/History/InnovThruIntra.html.
16. "Movers & Shakers 2014," *Library Journal* (March 10, 2014), http://lj.libraryjournal.com/2014/03/people/movers-shakers-2014/movers-shakers-2014/.
17. Bill Creech, *The Five Pillars of TQM: How to Make Total Quality Management Work for You* (New York: Truman Talley Books/Plume, 1994), 320. This quote is often attributed to the playwright George Bernard Shaw.

18. Daniel Boone Regional Library, "Vision, Mission, Values & Goals," 2016, http://www.dbrl.org/about/vision-mission-values-goals.

19. Cleveland State University, Michael Schwartz Library, "Library Mission, Purpose & Vision Statements," 2016, http://library.csuohio.edu/informa tion/mission.html.

20. Oak Park, Illinois, Public Library, "Mission & Vision," http://oppl.org/about/mission-vision.

21. Steely Library, Northern Kentucky University, "Library Administration," 2016, http://library.nku.edu/aboutthelibrary/libraryadministration.html.

22. Seth Godin, "The Rejectionists," Seth's blog, June 29, 2015, http://sethgo din.typepad.com/seths_blog/2015/06/the-rejectionists.html.

23. Irving L. Janis, *Victims of Groupthink: A Psychological Study of Foreign-Policy Decisions and Fiascoes* (Boston: Houghton Mifflin, 1972), 14.

24. Jerry B. Harvey, "The Abilene Paradox: The Management of Agreement," *Organizational Dynamics* 3 (Summer 1974) 63–80. CRM Learning released an excellent video titled *Abilene Paradox, Communication Training, Organization Behaviors, Accountability*, 2nd ed., and it is well worth a look. In one scenario, people admit that the idea of turning peanut oil into jet fuel is an "albatross," but the project is considered a "sacred cow" until one man stands up and says it won't work. All participants are relieved that the project is killed. In another, a man and woman agree to marry, but they really don't want to. They find the courage to say "no" at the altar. Video preview is available on YouTube; purchase information at CRM's Web site, http://www.crmlearning.com/Abilene-Paradox-P54388 .aspx.

25. Leslie Kwoh, "You Call That Innovation? Companies Love to Say They Innovate, but the Term Has Begun to Lose Meaning," *The Wall Street Journal*, May 23, 2012, http://www.wsj.com/articles/SB10001424052702 304791704577418250902309914.

26. Jeff Dyer and Hal Gregersen, "Are You an Innovative Entrepreneur? *Forbes*, June 4, 2012, http://www.forbes.com/sites/innovatorsdna/2012/ 06/04/are-you-an-innovative-entrepreneur/.

27. Russell Raath, "When Innovation Fails," *Forbes*, June 28, 2012, http:// www.forbes.com/sites/johnkotter/2012/06/28/the-leaders-path-to-inno vation-less-control-more-chaos/.

28. Kevin C. DeSouza, *Intrapreneurship: Managing Ideas within Your Organization* (Toronto: University of Toronto Press, 2011), 220.

29. Chris Messina, "The Full-Stack Employee," *Medium*, https://medium .com/@chrismessina/the-full-stack-employee-ed0db089f0a1.

30. Judy Panek and Ursula Pottinga, *Create a New Normal* ([N.p.]: Lulu, 2007), 42.

31. *Chambers Journal of Popular Literature: Science and Arts* (London: W. & R. Chambers, 1879), 598.

Calling All Change Agents: Creating an Intrapreneurial Culture at Your Library

Perhaps the greatest thing about this form of enabled intrapreneurship is that often everyone becomes so immersed in what they're doing that they feel like they own their companies. They don't feel like employees working for someone else, they feel much more like . . . well, I think the only word to describe it is "belongers."

—Richard Branson, Virgin Group[1]

There has to be a climate in which new ways of thinking, perceiving, questioning are encouraged. People also have to feel needed. Frequently, we just offer a job and "perks." We don't always offer people a purpose, a need for being there to use their skills and creativity.

—Maya Angelou[2]

In most organizations people are thought to be either dreamers or doers. Both talents are not generally required in one job. . . . A mind is meant to imagine and then act. It is a terrible thing to split apart the dreamer and the doer.

—Gifford Pinchot[3]

Creating a Culture of Intrapreneurship

Leaders, administrators, managers, and employees all have the ability to create a culture of innovation in the workplace that encourages intrapreneurial activities. A positive culture supports change agents who want to improve upon daily tasks, take ownership for ideas, attempt calculated risks, work within the system's organizational culture, and be inspired to go beyond the mundane. While those in authority in hierarchical organizations have the power to create a transparent, innovative culture, they also have the ability to demand obedience and stifle creativity at all levels. In other cases, supervisors may be fearful of allowing much innovation because they perceive that the organization as a whole ties their hands and they are simply not able to make changes. At the employee level, jealousy and fear can cause interpersonal conflicts that can stress out and disillusion potentially productive people.

How can a culture of intrapreneurship and a support for sustainable innovation be embedded in your organization? It requires diligence and understanding on the part of all employees—those who supervise and those who do not—managers, leaders, and administrators. All must make an effort to see beyond their own positions, be astute enough to pull innovation into overall goals and objectives, be willing to hire people who may know more than they do in certain areas, effectively cover costs (both monetary and through staffing changes), be transparent, work with others at all levels in a collegial fashion, both within, and frequently outside of the organization, and be willing to accept risk, even the risk of failure.

Remember too that all organizations have their own unique culture. The organizational culture influences how people act, work, and relate within the organization. Basically, culture is determined by the organization's shared assumptions, perceptions, values, beliefs, behaviors, language, and ethics, which govern how people in that organization act while on the job, including, but not limited to, dress, speech, and overall attitude. An organization's culture governs all of its social and professional framework, rules, and aspirations. It is the organization's shared values (see Figure 4.1).

Put simply, a library's culture directly affects how innovative it can be. Consider it the answer to "How do we do things around here?" The overall culture can encourage or discourage change agents, bring people together or alienate them, inspire the library to achieve its mission or to descend into mediocrity.

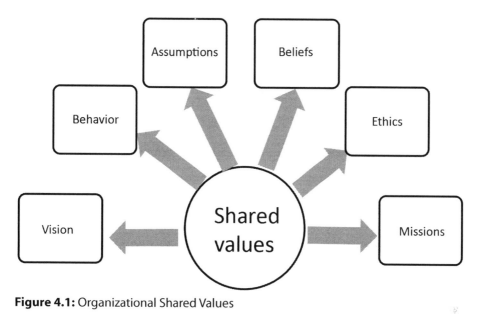

Figure 4.1: Organizational Shared Values

Potential change agents should read and fully understand the library's vision and mission statements to comprehend the self-perceived goals and imperatives of the organization (see Figure 4.2). Then, they should ask and answer several questions to better understand their library's culture. In addition, potential employees could also ask and get answers to these questions when interviewing for a new job.

1. Does the performance evaluation process reward, allow for, or dissuade employee innovations?

2. How does the organization handle employee mistakes? Is a certain level of risk tolerated?

3. How does the organization promote and encourage internal team development, both within departments and across departments as well as externally in the community?

4. How does my position support the organization's mission?

5. What kinds of diversity are present, not just in terms of people, but of environments, opinions, clothing styles, services?

6. How do the employees treat customers? Do they uniformly go the extra mile to provide superior service?

7. How do employees treat each other? Do they show respect and collegiality? How much backstabbing goes on when the target is not present? Are bullies allowed to thrive?

Jessica Ralli, coordinator of early literacy programs at the Brooklyn Public Library (New York City) and Rachel Payne, BPL's coordinator of early childhood services, combined intrapreneurial forces to create a texting program for participants in the library's popular Ready, Set, Kindergarten! (RSK) program designed to promote early literacy and school readiness. According to Ralli and Payne, one of the main goals of RSK emphasized engaging parents to adopt early literacy practices at home as part of their daily schedules. They wanted to connect with parents as effectively as possible and, based on research, opted for texting as the best solution.

Why texting? Ralli and Payne explain: "People open the messages more often than email/social media, they often have their phones on them, and many lower income families who may not have Internet access do have phones with texting capacity. We just had to try it!" The project came to light during a meeting of the City's First Readers (CFR) team, a citywide early literacy initiative funded by the NY City Council. When discussing how best to coordinate messaging, BPL's VP of Marketing and Communications, Robin Lester-Kenton, noted that the library's SMS service, which informed clients about holds, overdue books, and other issues, was underused. BPL had not reached its text limit. Essentially this free option for an improved service prompted a pilot project.

Ralli and Payne were encouraged to think outside the box while they explored a variety of options. Since Ralli's position at BPL was grant-funded through the CFR initiative, she was the logical choice to take the lead. Since she also managed RSK it was easy for her to connect with library staff, facilitators, and library users. As Ralli remarked, "It definitely took extra time, but was very much connected to the work I was already doing. Some of the librarians that support the RSK program helped me with the texting content, and I also used the tips and activities already tied to the curriculum we use." Although there were some technical questions about the new program, administration and staff supported the effort.

One finding of the pilot program was their discovery that clients were more willing to sign up for a trusted program supported by the library and carrying the library's brand name rather than a program unrelated to the library. "In the context of our programs, where patrons know the facilitators, librarians, and the content, they are willing (and excited) to sign up to receive more information." Ralli and Payne are working on ways to further expand the program including texting in different languages and obtaining feedback from participants. When asked if they considered themselves intrapreneurs, Ralli replied: "I admittedly had to look up 'intrapreneur!' I ran my own business for seven years, so I think I naturally approach certain things with that spirit of entrepreneurship, even when within a larger organization. I love the idea of implementing great ideas right away in a small and manageable way to learn more about their potential, and I think BPL really supports that. I think all educators and librarians are change agents, so yes!" Check out the solution at http://www.bklynlibrary.org/first-5-years/ready-set-kindergarten-english.

Figure 4.2: Change Agent in Action[4]

8. Are employees encouraged to see the big picture? To see beyond their own department and position, both internally and externally?

9. What is the general decision-making style in the organization?

10 Is the culture open or fearful? If fearful, what appears to be the cause?

11. Do employees have a positive or negative attitude toward their jobs, each other, managers, and the overall administration? Why or why not?

Individual employees often have good ideas, but in order to bring those ideas from conception to completion, they need the approval and support of their supervisors, managers, peers, and sometimes their clientele. Some ways in which managers can create and foster these ideas and create an intrapreneurial win-win culture are to

- encourage and empower individuals by listening to their ideas and soliciting solutions;

- form cross-departmental teams to address particular needs, take advantage of opportunities, and consider new services;

- serve as mentors and sponsors;

- work through political battles (bring out the big guns) to support a worthwhile project that includes organizational change that may be viewed as radical by other employees or other administrators;

- assume the risk of navigating through cumbersome regulations to help intrapreneurs achieve success for the organization;

- provide resources needed to develop an idea and its solution, both internally and externally: provide resources in the form of staff, facilities, materials, money, networking;

- avoid the just-do-the-job-and-shut-up syndrome even when you are too busy to think straight;

- remain inclusive and support employees as important ingredients in the overall recipe of the organization: let them know that they are truly important to the organization;

- disseminate policies and encourage positive and productive discussion;

- empower frontline staff to make decisions that positively impact service to clientele based on knowledge and approved policy;

- provide a reward structure outside of the bureaucratic system, such as anonymously putting small gifts and thank-you notes on desks, creating an employee-of-the-month award, fostering interactions at catered luncheons and other gatherings, providing time flexibility and autonomy for projects within the parameters of labor laws;

- direct and encourage an individual's talents toward organizational goals;

- offer training opportunities both within and outside of the organization;

- lead by example, put on a happy face, assume rose-colored glasses, promote optimism even in the face of budget difficulties, be enthusiastic about your job, and encourage others to do the same;

- be transparent in terms of strategies, budgets, and, as much as possible, personnel decisions;

- be passionate about leading and creating new opportunities for employees to expand their ability to be creative and to make more money, for example, teaching or taking classes, consulting, serving on outside boards, joining service organizations;

- never ever say "It's not my job!" but instead say "we're all in this together" and ask "what we can do together to make this happen?";

- guide conflict into a positive, not negative, conclusion, serve as a facilitator and, if necessary, referee and take action to counter abusive practices;

- encourage employees to see opportunities and target them as leaders for new innovations by letting them chair committees but be ever vigilant not to let bullies run rampant;

- modify the performance appraisal process as organizational policies allow to encourage and reward intrapreneurial activities;

- be alert to the effects of creative destruction and look for ways to redirect resources while maintaining employee self-esteem.

Managers attuned to the organization's culture are aware that good and not so good ideas are generated on a daily basis. Teams form and dissolve, make recommendations, spend time productively or waste time inefficiently, achieve sustainable results or fail to agree on any recommendation at all. Oftentimes, employees want to see a change, blame managers for being roadblocks, but do not want to work through the process themselves. How many times have managers heard "I have this great idea and we really need to change our procedures to make it work" or "I was chatting with John the other day and he suggested that we change the entire process of how we buy materials" but see no solutions forthcoming. In an innovative environment, employees have as much responsibility as managers to make innovation happen.

Supporting a Culture of Innovation-Employees

"Because it has always been this way." That's a pretty bad answer to a series of common questions. . . . The real answer is, "Because if someone changes it, that someone will be responsible for what happens." Are you okay with that being the reason things are the way they are?

—Seth Godin[5]

Will you, the employee, take the responsibility and bear the burden of consequences for an idea? That is what Godin says in his quote above. You have to take responsibility for the changes because you are not content with business as usual. Godin makes other points in his book *Linchpin: Are You Indispensable*, where he discusses freely giving the gift of emotional labor: the smile, the extra help, the enthusiasm, the real interest for your job. He encourages all members of an organization to consider themselves artists in the general sense of the word "art," being "anything that's creative, passionate, and personal."[6] Such artists are at work in libraries, stores, factories, government offices, schools; they can be anywhere that humans interact. Art reflects your intent, your ability to communicate. Personal and creative, your intent to better your job creates value not only for you, but for those you work with and for. You can create change in others simply by remaining positive.

Art as emotional labor is not easy, nor does it come risk-free, but it can successfully support your efforts as an organizational change agent because it makes other individuals change their attitudes. It is human interaction at its best. It reflects the admonition to do something productive today. For example, positive results by positive and empowered frontline staff can calm a distraught mother who has just received a $50 bill for her children's supposedly lost books. Taking personal responsibility and offering solutions on the front line can go a long way to promote positive responses for all concerned. Do everything you can even while you acknowledge the rules governing your actions within the organization.

Finally, do not succumb to victimhood. Victims, whiners, negative people, and fearful employees are not optimistic employees and cannot be truly effective change agents. Avoid saying, "It's not my job." Doing a job that needs to be done should be your job. If not you, then who? Refuse to satisfice. Doing the bare minimum is not enough. Make a difference in your organization.

Pick Your Battles: When You Have to Work within a Specific Structure

Everyone likes to innovate, change, and make things better along with a free rein to do so, but as employees of an organization that is larger than yourself, you need to conform to certain parameters. These may include strategic initiatives, directives set by levels of administration above you, policies, laws, contracts, and work rules. The successful intrapreneur functions within these structures, pushing the envelope and creating change by convincing others and by building collaborations and partnerships. Positive change results in new services, improved work flows, more efficient use of resources, and satisfied clientele.

Move carefully; yours may not be the only way. Running roughshod over others and being unwilling to compromise or using crude or naïve attempts at politicking will produce negative results both for the library and the employee. It will produce organizational turmoil, resulting in deterioration of services, and could even cause you and your supportive colleagues your remove and their jobs! Even when such an approach creates an opportunity to make a change, your credibility may be lost, thereby damaging or removing future opportunities.

To be most effective in the intrapreneurial role, it is important to develop an understanding of how organizational structure works, including the roles and practice of administrators. Having some knowledge of managerial practice will help you to better understand the reasons for certain decisions and may also help you to develop approaches to more effectively answer concerns. A good, general library management book, such as the latest edition of Moran, Stueart and Morner's classic text *Library and Information Center Management*[7] will provide you with a concise, easy-to-understand explanation of the managerial decision-making process.

Developing a technical understanding of the proper role and function of management will help you in the development of another critical skill: the ability to empathize with people who work at various levels within the organization, including peers, subordinates, and superiors. Often, the natural tendency is to dehumanize those whom we do not understand. Dehumanizing is incredibly unproductive. It prevents us for seeing possibilities for improving communication and developing understanding that may improve the opportunities for acceptance of our ideas. Thinking or stating some unexplained and perhaps unfounded reason for a disagreement prevents you from analyzing the situation and coming up with ways to persuade people to see things your way. Empathy and working to understand the possible reasons for a negative answer, maintaining a positive attitude, and being open to modifications of your idea can turn a "no" into a "maybe" or a "yes, with conditions."

Similarly, as we find in the Kenny Rogers song, you need to "know when to hold 'em and know when to fold 'em."[8] That is, carefully choose your battles. Not every battle is worth fighting. In military history, many combatants have won the battle but lost the war. Pushing every idea, innovation, or concern to the maximum will build stress on you and others and seriously damage your credibility with supervisors and colleagues. In the short term, you may be able to force an item or two through. In the long run, you will damage your working relationships and reduce your chance of building support for future changes. If you run into resistance or rejection, take a sober and realistic look at your idea. Truly, how important is acceptance of the particular idea? Is it, in fact, the best approach for a solution? What will be the results to the organization if the idea is rejected? Think the issue through and be prepared to make a reasoned, cognizant argument rather than an impromptu attempt.[9] Prioritize and realize that it might be well worth it to sacrifice an idea from time to time rather than to be seen as a curmudgeon who cannot take a "no" for an answer.

What happens when your great idea is accepted but doesn't really work? This is part of the implementation and assessment process discussed in later chapters. Be aware, however, that not every great idea yields a great return. Sometimes taking the time to evaluate your idea objectively after implementation can lead to a better idea. Sometimes you have to drop an idea because it simply does not work out well. Sometimes ideas get tangled up in red tape and come out mangled, and then you may have to step in and destroy the entire project. In any event, it's like falling off a bicycle: get back on and continue riding.

Competitive Advantage

Remaining positive and striving to create an intrapreneurial culture promotes and enhances your organization's competitive advantage. Libraries are no longer the only purveyors of information. In today's world, services offered in libraries must outperform those offered by their competitors, and libraries must enhance their competitive advantage. A library's competitive advantage is maintaining quality, innovation, responsiveness, and efficiency for its clients, thereby generating value. Libraries need to be recognized for the value of the financial investment made in them by their users or the public. Libraries need to use all available resources, including the empowerment of change agents, to compete and respond to new needs, opportunities, and challenges quickly and efficiently.

Competition is not limited to the for-profit world, nor it is as simple as a non-profit rephrasing its mission statement. All organizations, whether they serve the public good or are interested in achieving wealth, are in competition for a share of a market that includes service to, and rewards from, customers and potential donors.[10]

Consider the factors necessary to achieve competitive advantage, while recognizing that all actions must be timely in nature. Do not settle for the status quo. Make ideas into opportunities, not chores. Do not fall into the trap of taking an attitude of professional purity by rejecting business practices because they were created outside of the library world. Similarly, be open to partnerships with individuals and groups from various professions and businesses, including those who do not have "MLS" after their names. Take the best from business and entrepreneurship and use it to further the library profession and your library's services. American librarian and knowledge services specialist Guy St. Clair discussed barriers to excellence and concluded that "the library product cannot be dismissed as merely another ephemeral bureaucratic service delivered by practitioners when convenient."[11] Librarians should not be afraid to be entrepreneurial lest it "somehow prevent us from being the admired moral leaders we've been led to believe others think we are . . . or that we ourselves think we are."[12] Libraries do prove their value to their constituents through honest evaluation and promotion. It is part of a library's competitive advantage, as illustrated in Figure 4.3.

Once you acknowledge that competition can breed opportunity and is a real part of a non-profit's culture, work through the overcoming-obstacles worksheet (see Figure 4.4) and think about how you can

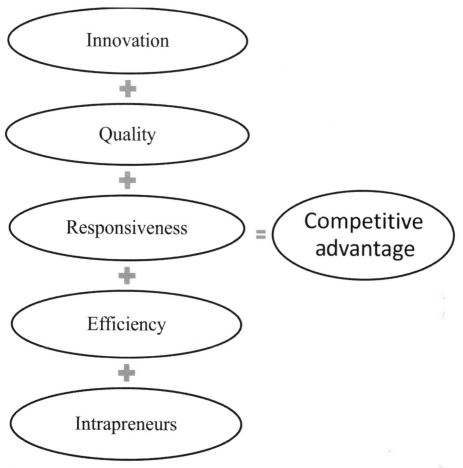

Figure 4.3: Competitive Advantage Chart

best provide solutions and create an intrapreneurial culture in your organization.

Recognize, understand, and accept obstacles, but don't let them keep you from innovating. While a healthy intrapreneurial environment can certainly come from the top, don't let that stop you from contributing to a nurturing environment for innovation at all levels. The spirit to innovate comes from each intrapreneur; it is an internal need. Remember that libraries that promote and support intrapreneurial activities better serve their clientele than those that do not. Be that innovator, take those risks, label your competition, be proactive, and be transformative. Be your organization's intrapreneur and successful change agent.

Potential Obstacles	Analysis and Solutions
How do performance evaluations encourage a culture of innovation in your library? If not, how might they be changed?	
Does every employee understand his or her responsibilities and how to most effectively meet performance expectations?	
Are employees given opportunities to discuss obstacles to their successful performance? If yes, how? If no, why?	
Are employees encouraged to request help in the form of training or flexibility in schedule?	
How may employees make suggestions for work place improvements?	
How do managers or supervisors communicate with employees and keep them informed of issues?	
How do managers or supervisors and the organization's administration recognize and acknowledge employee achievement?	
How are managers or supervisors made aware of workplace issues and obstacles that can potentially prevent an employee or a department from working effectively?	
If issues arise, such as bullying, negativity, or lack of participation, how do supervisors address the issue so that others are not adversely affected by the behaviors?	
When your administration requests feedback, do you take the initiative to understand the issue then do research and provide useful feedback?	
How often do you offer realistic suggestions based on the organizations strategic goals?	
How do you handle "no?" Do you perceive this as an obstacle or an opportunity? Why?	
Lack of funds: opportunity or threat? Has your library looked at alternate funding methods? Grants? Corporate sponsorships? Friends of the Library initiatives? Partnerships with local businesses or other nonprofit groups?	
Do too many goals limit innovation? Are your goals unrealistic or realistic?	
What long-range organization plans stifle or encourage productivity and creativity?	

Figure 4.4: Overcoming Obstacles Worksheet

Notes

1. Richard Branson, "Richard Branson on Intrapreneurs," *Entrepreneur*, January 31, 2011, http://www.entrepreneur.com/article/218011.
2. Jeffrey M. Elliot, ed., *Conversations with Maya Angelou* (Jackson: University Press of Mississippi, 1989), x.
3. Gifford Pinchot, "Innovation through Intrapreneuring," *Research Management* 20, no. 2 (March–April 1987), Intraapreneur.com, http://www.intra preneur.com/MainPages/History/InnovThruIntra.html.
4. Rachel Payne and Jessica Ralli, e-mail messages to authors, July 2015.
5. Seth Godin, "Because It Has Always Been This Way," http://sethgodin .typepad.com/seths_blog/2015/07/because-it-has-always-been-this-way .html.
6. Seth Godin, *Linchpin: Are You Indispensable* (New York: Portfolio, 2010), 83.
7. Barbara B. Moran, Robert D. Stueart, and Claudia J. Morner, *Library and Information Center Management*, 8th ed. (Santa Barbara, CA: Libraries Unlimited, 2014).
8. Kenny Rogers, "The Gambler" (1978). AZLyrics.com, c2000–2016, http://www.azlyrics.com/lyrics/kennyrogers/thegambler.html.
9. Lee Anna Jackson, "Be a Good Politician," *Black Enterprise* (2004): 186, http://search.proquest.com/abiglobal/docview/217905890/fulltext/52304C 2478A64A96PQ/2?accountid=12817.
10. Mollie West and Andy Posner, "Defining Your Competitive Advantage: All Social Change Organizations Have One, But Yours May Not Be What You Think It Is," *Stanford Social Innovation Review*, January 23, 2013, http:// www.ssireview.org/blog/entry/defining_your_competitive_advantage.
11. Guy St. Clair, *Entrepreneurial Librarianship: The Key to Effective Information Services Management* (London: Bowker Saur, 1996), 1.
12. Ibid., p. xxii.

CHAPTER 5

The Intrapreneurial Process: Finding the Way to Success

Every new idea . . . evokes three stages of reaction:
It's impossible. Don't waste my time
It's possible, but it's not worth doing
I said it was a good idea all along
The intrapreneur successfully manages these barriers to convert a promising idea into a sustainable innovation.

—Peter Cook[1]

In this chapter we begin the process of finding your way to a successful innovation. It is the heart and soul of being an intrapreneur and making successful change within your organization. Working through ideas is a process, one that you may perform individually or within a team setting or, preferably, both. There are always barriers to any innovation, as we have seen in previous chapters, such as the intrapreneur's concern about her time, her ability to promote the idea, and her fear of failure, budget issues, internal and external influences. Putting all these aside, however, it is time to examine the steps to success. In this chapter we will explore the following questions:

- Ideas and brainstorming: Where do I begin?
- Client-needs assessment: Gathering information.

- Thinking through ideas: Fine tune concepts.
- Creating your own future: Outside the box, outside the building.
- SCAMPER: Create, modify, expand your idea.
- Distilling an idea because *all ideas are not created equal.*
- Define value and express the idea.
- Screening, research, and feasibility study: Getting your ducks in a row.
- Feasibility study.

Ideas and Brainstorming

Finding a solution requires a different perspective than the one you used to define the problem. It also requires a different brain state. The creative problem-solving activity is a completely different brain function from the analytical problem-defining activity.

—Dixie Gillaspie[2]

You have ideas, see opportunities, and perceive needs. You want to get started in making a difference to better lives through a specific new or modified service. You see possibilities to change a current service or you are not sure your existing services are adequately offering solutions for your clientele. You are reacting to several serious and legitimate complaints about the quality of one of your services. In another instance, you attended a meeting and returned with great ideas and possible solutions for enhancing services. Recently, you have taken classes and explored new and different ways to innovate. You chatted with your sister who asked why your library seemed to be avoiding a service for a specific group. You have the opportunity to partner with a community organization to create a center to help the underserved in your area. Your library has suffered from an unplanned disaster, such as a flood or a fire, and you now have the opportunity to change everything. The need for innovation comes from both internal and external sources. What do you do now?

Settling on an idea and then shepherding it through the filtering and approval process are key components of a change agent's repertoire. Admittedly, some ideas, devices, and services may fail; that is all part of the risk process. But that only brings us fully back to the idea that if you don't try you will never succeed.

A change agent's main role is to facilitate meaningful change that will help the organization. The old adage "It is better to ask for forgiveness than for permission" should not be part of a change agent's vocabulary.

It implies that the change agent is a sole agent, acting on his own and using the organization's time and money to do what he thinks is best. It implies that others are left out of the communication loop. It means a lack of consideration and respect for others. Change agents must be savvy and considerate enough to work with and through others. They must examine, understand, and comprehend the organization's big picture, which shows where the organization wants to go and how everyone fits into that vision, whether they are employees, administrators, or clientele. Consider also the following: what if you are not forgiven? You have damaged your credibility and ability to be an effective change agent. You may also have damaged your ability to work well with your colleagues, both internal and external.

Given that loose cannons run over people to the detriment of all, where do you begin? Start by building your knowledge. This will allow you to form a strategic perspective, which will, in turn, allow you to develop ideas that will better mesh with the mission of your organization and the beliefs and ideals of your coworkers. As stated in earlier chapters, know your organization's mission and vision statements, trends in the library and information profession, technological innovations that can aid your work, and the people you serve. Obtain and analyze statistical and other descriptive information from your organization in the area in which you have a particular interest. Once you have developed a deeper understanding of the situation and have a broad, strategic outlook, you are better prepared to move on to the idea generation phase.

Start by sharpening your ax as you begin to travel the innovation road with a project in mind. Consider the much-related story of a woodcutter. Being offered a job he fell to his task with gusto. The first week he chopped down 18 trees. In the second week, working just as fast and hard, he only chopped down 11 trees. By the third week, working constantly and totally exhausted, he only felled 5 trees. What decreased the productivity of the woodcutter? Was he getting weaker? The woodcutter asked his boss about the issue. His boss replied: "Have you sharpened your ax?" The woodcutter thought for a moment, and then responded: "I haven't had any time to sharpen my ax. I've been too busy chopping wood."[3]

We often forget to sharpen our ax. We fall into a routine that becomes a rut. We concentrate exclusively on our day-to-day tasks to an extent that we feel that we do not have time to be creative or innovative. Do you find yourself in the situation of being overwhelmingly bound to day-to-day activities? Do you answer "yes" most of the time? This problem is similar to that of people who never seem to be able to save money. Financial experts advise people to save first, before paying bills, as the one sure way to build wealth. In a similar sense, you need to schedule dedicated *creative time* within the workday, and then make sure to truly reserve that time for creative thinking. Take an honest look at recurring tasks and apply some of your creativity to redesigning your own work flow. Delegate so that you do not spend most of your day putting out fires and being the only problem solver in your area. Are there tasks and decisions which you can delegate to another individual? Through this empowerment, you can free up some creative time for yourself. Consider which work flows or services are no longer relevant that can be swept away to make room for potential new improvements. Alternately, are you using mundane tasks as an excuse to avoid spending time on potential improvements or new services? Are you procrastinating? Are you retaining tasks that you enjoy, tasks that could be done more effectively by others? Be strict with yourself and actively work to avoid allowing your recurring tasks, need to control, or feelings of inadequacy to infringe on creative time. Take the time to think and strategize rather than simply to react. Know how to think, not what to think. Finally, work smarter, not harder. To that end, let's look at some tools that can help to inspire, sharpen, and finally hone your ax of successful innovation.

Client Needs Assessment—"Information, We Want Information"[4]

> See the Big Picture. Aim beyond the moon and never let perfect get in the way of good.
>
> —Arne J. Almquist

One source of inspiration for the budding intrapreneur is your users. How do you know what your users really want from your organization? You ask them. One way is to perform a needs assessment. Of course, sometimes users don't even know what they should be asking for. Did computer users know they needed the Macintosh before it came to market? Ditto for the iPhone. Users wanted a portable computer, but were not sure of the details. Enter the professionals. It is a useful first step to solicit feedback from both internal and external clients to enhance the idea generation process. After all, what is a product if it does not meet someone's needs, even needs they may not yet know they have?

The American Library Association includes some insightful information in starting dialogs in its brief publication *How Librarians and Libraries Can Lead Community Conversations for Change: A Conversation Guide*, in which it recommends ways to engage people according to their aspirations, to find a way to come together to get things done, to bring together diverse groups and to see what they have in common, as well as to build "deeper relationships within the broader community." [5]

A good first place to look is the suggestion box, webpage blog, social media, or other feedback sources. Most libraries maintain a mechanism for soliciting user input, whether these are complaints, praise, or requests for new products or services. These resources are excellent conduits for new product/service suggestions. Often, the user will express a perceived need in the form of a request for a specific item or service. Consider that request carefully and determine the actual need. Is it really the item or service the user requested or something else? As a professional, you add value to any decision, and being able to distinguish between a specific request and an overall need is a significant consideration. Using your knowledge of your organization and clientele, your professional expertise, and your experience, you can and should make that decision. Then you explore how to go beyond it.

Going beyond the obvious, consider the case of Shanika Heyward.[6] Using her library's strategic plan as a guide, she wanted to increase library use. To that end, she worked with community groups to move beyond the library and establish such events as "Breakfast with a Cop." She also partnered with the Washington Township Adult Education Program to provide a "GED teacher, job coach, and teacher assistant for weekly classes."[7] Heyward certainly embodies a successful change agent as well as embraces her library's vision: "to be a center of knowledge, community life and innovation for Indianapolis."[8]

Like Shanika, maintain your focus and strive to remain positive as you move through the innovation process. As you solicit feedback, keep in mind one caveat: accumulating complaints is easy. The key is to sift through complaints to determine the true issue and take appropriate action so that by the time you address a complaint the individual who had the problem is neither too angry to care or has given up hope of a solution. In addition, one complaint may actually represent the negative experiences of multiple users since many others will simply leave rather than bother to complain. That said, a thoughtful examination of user complaints can start you on the road to developing ideas and solutions.

On another note, community push back, in terms of anti-tax groups, can be turned into positive support if you take the time to meet people on their own terms. That is what Lance Werner, executive director of the Kent District Library in Comstock Park, Michigan, did. He needed a

45 percent increase in library millage or the system would close. Well-meaning advocates advised him to avoid direct contact with anti-tax groups, but Werner met the challenge head on instead. He recognized that many opponents had legitimate points. So Werner presented his case to the groups. He noted: "They asked tough questions, and we answered them. [W]e all came away with a greater understanding of each other." Werner even turned one opponent into a supporter. "I learned that people are people, and it is a mistake to make assumptions. We managed to find a library champion that was anything but obvious."[9]

Direct contacts, community interactions, listening to concerns are all valid ways to collect information. Another common technique is to conduct a needs assessment study. This can take the form of a survey, telephone interviews, focus groups, or any combination of the above. The Via Christi Regional Medical Center Libraries in Wichita, Kansas, conducted a needs assessment to serve as the basis of their strategic plan. Their study included a self-reporting survey which appeared in both print and web-based versions. Besides the fixed response questions, an open-ended question was appended to the end of the survey. The fixed response questions allowed librarians to acquire information based on their expectations. The open-ended question gave users a chance to bring forward ideas in a freer, unstructured manner.[10]

Surveys can provide a quick, easy, and low-impact method for obtaining user input. They can be created and distributed very inexpensively. Print survey forms can be placed in accessible areas, such as a literature rack or service desk. Employees can provide users with the survey instruments as a part of their normal service transactions. Online surveys can be made available using low- or no-cost solutions such as Survey Monkey. Data can be readily analyzed using methods ranging from extremely simple (lists) to sophisticated statistical analysis. Even in cases where a statistically significant sample cannot be obtained, surveys can provide the innovator with useful data which may be used to suggest new innovations. Keep in mind, however, the impersonal nature of most surveys as well as the mathematicians' joke that statistics are only as good as the person faking them. You want information, not faked facts. Never rely on surveys alone as the basis for your innovation.

Consider these issues when creating your survey.

1. Unsuitable and confusing questions
   a. Avoid using professional jargon or labels that mean something only to the employees, including abbreviations, acronyms, and

initialisms: "how effective is our MARC cataloging in helping you to complete a Boolean search in our OCLC online catalog?"

b. Badly worded sentences combined with questions that people may not want to answer can limit responses: "what is your age?"

c. Avoid leading questions, that is, questions that, through their wording, influence or determine outcomes to support already-determined conclusions: "how did our well-received and publicly-supported service meet your needs?" Instead, remove any words that could sway a respondent: "did this service meet your needs?"

2. Wrong people

a. Determine who you wish to survey and why. If not effectively targeted, you may obtain useless data from the wrong group of users.

3. Wrong time

a. The issue is not yet seen as an issue, or there is little urgency for solving the issue. Timing is important; otherwise potential respondents will not feel a need to contribute.

4. Wrong issues

a. Like picking the right time for the survey, you must emphasize the important issues and not become bogged down with irrelevant questions.

5. Unclear outcomes

a. Make sure you know what you want from the survey. Why are you even doing it?

6. Overlong surveys

a. Just give me 10 minutes, the survey entreats: Why? Are you kidding? How many of us have 10 minutes to spare? Don't assume your users do either.

7. A prize for completing the survey

a. Not a bad idea if the drawing is for something popular with your clientele. Of course, many people respond to surveys simply to get something for nothing and this hardly makes their responses noteworthy. As noted in point 2 above, make sure you are surveying the people who can give you the most useful feedback.

Ideally, surveys might include just five or fewer fixed response questions with a rating such as "How likely are you to recommend the Wubsville Public Library to a friend?" and no more than two open-ended questions, which allows respondents to explain what they like or dislike in their own words. Surveys do not have to be boring. They can be fun and centered on a new promotion, exhibit, or event in the library or community. However, you accumulate survey responses, make sure to provide feedback to the respondents so they know that their voice has been heard. In preparing surveys, check out resources available online free of cost.[11]

How else might you elicit information? Talk to your clientele. Depending on your needs and use of the data, this can be done in an informal setting or through a focus group. A focus group moves the information-gathering process into the realm of qualitative research. Keep the group relatively small and select individuals who are representative of the larger population. Ask questions that help to determine attitudes, identify problems, or explore potential solutions to problems.

Focus groups can provide an excellent way to gauge the attitudes and opinions of your users and to identify problems that can be addressed through the development of innovative solutions. John Ledingham and Stephen Bruning, in "Ten Tips for Better Focus Groups," suggest keeping your focus group size to about 6 to 10 members. If the group size is too small, you won't get diversity of opinion. If it is too large, the group becomes less manageable. You should approach the group with a well thought-out strategy, that is, some structure, rather than simply fishing for answers. The authors find that it is often better to use an experienced moderator from outside of the library. In a college or university setting, you may be able to tap the resources of the college or department of business or the campus marketing unit. Public libraries may be able to solicit expertise from a local college or university, a large business, an independent marketing expert, or marketing/research people working for the parent organization. You may be able to find someone willing to provide their expertise pro bono or as a gift-in-kind. Use of someone from outside of the library should alleviate the possibility of creating leading questions or the introduction of biases from library employees who may be less than impartial or worse, defensive.[12]

In addition, Ledingham and Bruning recommend recording the sessions on video, with written permission from the participants. This allows those unable to attend a live session an opportunity to observe and experience the non-verbal reactions of the group. They also suggest that the process of editing a 2-hour session into a 15-minute video summary can provide a message that is very different from that possible with a written summary or report.[13]

As part of the process here and in marketing (see Chapter 8 for marketing your service or product), consider the needs of your clientele. Why do they use your service or the library as a whole? What are their needs: immediate, long-term, perceived, and those currently unrecognized? Use the needs worksheet in Figure 5.1 to help you sort out these issues and take a closer look at how you will offer a solution.

To understand client needs and the environment in which you work and provide service, put yourself in your client's shoes. Begin with a thorough understanding of your organization, its clientele, the community, and the social, economic, and cultural environment. Talk to your

---

Consider why your current and future clientele would use your service or product. Answer questions about immediate, long-term, perceived, and unperceived needs.

Define the service or product.

_____

What immediate needs does the service or product serve? These are things which are not currently provided by your library and are needed immediately.

_____

What long-term needs are served? These are products or services that are not desperately needed at present but will be needed at some point in the future.

_____

How does the product or service fulfill user-perceived needs? These are products or services for which your clientele perceive a need. Remember that perception can be just as powerful as reality.

_____

Does the service or product fulfill any needs that your clients haven't yet perceived? Innovations uncover or create needs your clientele didn't realize existed.

_____

Figure 5.1: Needs Worksheet

colleagues, clientele, and community leaders. And *listen* to their comments. Once you have information from your clientele, it is time to do some thinking of your own.

Thinking through Ideas

Ideas are easy. Implementation is hard. Keep thinking.

—Guy Kawasaki[14]

You know that your clientele and their needs have changed, but you continue to offer the same services and accept the same outcomes. Granted, some of those services still work just fine, but how well do they meet current needs? Do you simply satisfice, maintaining the status quo, or do you listen and make improvements? Consider brainstorming ideas, both individually and collectively. As you work through this process, you will find that some ideas work better than others. You will discover that different people are able to use specific methods more effectively than others. Overreaching are the needs of the people you serve, which demand that you respond. There are many ways to work toward a solution within your organization. One tried and true method is to brainstorm. But the conundrum remains. Which comes first, the need or the idea?

Generally needs stimulate ideas. Begin your innovation process with idea generation based on client and organizational needs and inputs. How do you start? One way is to facilitate ideas and comments from your colleagues or the people you serve, or both. Consider the best way to gather these ideas and adjust your plans accordingly.

Brainstorming sessions need to be open, interactive and productive. Sometimes they are not and this is where you, the intrapreneur, need to step in to fix the process. For example, picture yourself in a conference room with eight other people. A facilitator, who might be an outside consultant or one of your management team, asks you to generate as many ideas as you can in 15 minutes. She says that every idea is equal and that all ideas are valid. As you and the others struggle to formulate ideas, focus, and think, you are asked to generate ideas. The facilitator and her assistants write them on a board or you submit them on sticky notes. At the end of the 15 minutes, which seems like 15 hours, the ideas are posted. You now have to vote for the best ones—or the ones everyone else voted for. (Remember groupthink in Chapter 3!) You are rushed, stressed, confused, and wondering why you are there. You also think, "I had a great solution, but I can't get it worked out in this setting. I am pressured to agree with the others. No one sees what I see.

Besides, there is Betsy Blabbermouth who just won't shut up. Andy Arnickle is giving me the stare of death. Fred the naysayer is already attacking everything." What to do?

The key here, as elsewhere, is collegial collaboration. Don't derail your own ideas through self-doubt or allow another person to derail you because of his negativity. Change that facilitation session for the better. Ask to head a brainstorming session and create an environment where everyone feels comfortable presenting her ideas. Make it clear from the beginning that negative comments are not productive and all comments must come with constructive feedback. Let all participants know up front what the goals of the meeting are: to create and throw ideas around. Make it a collegial and productive experience. Make it a relaxed experience away from the demands of work for at least a few hours. Bring in some beverages and snacks. Create a comfortable, socially relaxed atmosphere. Above all consider: who will benefit from the ideas generated at the session. Remember, it may not even be your idea that comes forth as the most viable. Or your idea may be enhanced from others' comments. Begin, conduct, and conclude the session with respect.

Easier said than done, you say. As Kevin DeSouza notes, "it takes a community of believers within the organization to see an idea through the process of development."[15] Respectful change agents can be the start, the catalyst, for better communication. That is, find solutions if your participants' supervisors, including your own, balk at allowing an hour or two just to think. If you cannot arrange for an effective face-to-face brainstorming session, consider the option of digital brainstorming, which can be done at any time—even outside of working hours if necessary. In this method, participants may make comments and assess feedback at their convenience. Additionally, the asynchronous nature of digital communication allows you all to process ideas more fully by thinking first and writing second. This allows all participants to take some time to weigh and edit their comments. It allows you all to communicate on a group level while maintaining autonomy and the ability to think in the solitude of your own office or personal space. While this approach might more directly appeal to introverts, group work online allows creativity to flow yet reminds us to always take responsibility for our actions. Responsibility is the key and one procedure to avoid is anonymous comments. Anonymity can result in destructive behaviors, such as attacking and ridiculing others and their ideas. That is not a collegial or necessarily a successful way to go about brainstorming.

Another aspect of responsibility includes addressing and answering difficult questions. Sometimes we are so enamored of our idea that we forget about specific issues. Therefore, as part of the brainstorming sessions, and after you have completed the needs assessment, consider the following questions and answer them truthfully and fully while remembering that all innovations and changes need to be strategically aligned with your organization's goals.

- What are we trying to accomplish here?
- What will be the end result from our idea and solution?
- Who will benefit?
- How will this solution make my library a better place?
- Why am I inspired to complete this process?
- How does this fit in with my organization's goals?
- Who can help with this process?
- Why or why not am I the best person to implement this idea?

Creating Your Own Future

In many ways, innovative change is the best way an organization can create its own future, make products or services fresh again, and maintain relevance in a changing society. As part of the need for relevance, change may inspire innovative ideas for new or alternate ways to use existing products or services. Consider the saturated market for something as common as baking soda. As demands changed, there was not much demand for it in a world that did not bake extensively because baking soda was just for baking things, right? Wrong. Thinking outside of the box inspired creative changes in marketing that convinced people to use it for other purposes, such as to freshen a refrigerator or garbage disposal. In this way, the manufacturers re-marketed an old product stuck in a static market into one that had new and different uses. They successfully created another use for a vintage product and thereby effectively invented additional value for it.

What other innovations inspired by the need to change and grow are relevant to our discussion? Quite a few, as you can see in the list below.

- Technical innovator and officer in the US Navy, Rear Admiral Bradley Allen Fiske (1854–1942) envisioned a way to make reading more comfortable to those who wore glasses, and at the same time, reduce the physical size of books. The Fiske Reading Machine, introduced in 1922 (see Figure 5.2), consisted of a portable light,

The Fiske Reading Machine

Harris & Ewing Collection, Prints & Photographs Division, Library of Congress, LC-H27-A-4276. Published in Scientific American, June 1922. Public Domain. http://www.loc.gov/pictures/item/hec2013002191/

Figure 5.2: The Fiske Reading Machine

handheld magnifying glass, and a *comfort cover* for one eye. In essence, this was a roaring-twenties version of the e-readers of today. Besides the advantages listed above, Fiske believed that it would lower the cost of books, which were out of reach to the poor, it would provide the opportunity to produce books on higher-quality paper while still saving costs, and make the smaller books much cheaper to mail, again, lowering costs for a large portion of the population.[16]

■ Based on knowledge of your clientele, consider moving to purchases in electronic formats. Rather than having to come to a physical place to access materials as is the case with traditional content, e-book and other digital content gives your users the ability to access materials from wherever they have Internet access. As an added plus, digital loans automatically expire removing the need to physically return materials to the library.

■ The gas station/convenience store was a revolutionary innovation for its time. Libraries have long moved outside of their doors to bring books to people where the people could best access them. The mid-19th century saw the emergence of deposit station libraries, which were basically traveling libraries or collections that central libraries delivered to factories, stores, churches, post offices, nursing homes, jails, daycares, prisons, homeless shelters, schools, and just about anywhere else in urban or rural areas where there was a need. Shopkeepers, post office employees, or shop stewards created space for the books and crates, supervised checkout, and inventoried and maintained the collection. In 1874, the Chicago Public Library delivered books by horse-drawn carriage to library deposit stations in candy or drug stores.[17] Bookmobiles brought materials to suburban neighborhoods where one-car families in the 1950s and 1960s were confined. Many libraries still offer this service today through cybermobiles, adding online computer access to traditional book collections.

- Would your library take the delivery system one step farther by putting books into machines for clientele with a library card to check out? Several libraries have installed book-vending machines in key locations, such as shopping centers and bus and rail stations. California's Contra Costa County Library machines were part of the Library-a-Go-Go project starting in 2008–2009. While an innovative idea at the time, use of the machines has fallen off and circulation has dropped as the concept has been supplanted by the library's circulation of e-books.[18] This represents a clear example of a great idea in its time, but even more importantly demonstrates the need for continuous reevaluation and assessment.

- Want to capture books from local authors who self-publish? Check out SELF-e, a collaborative effort between *Library Journal* and BiblioBoard, which encourages local authors to promote their books through libraries and libraries to promote those books through access.[19] SELF-e offers a clear alternative to corporate publishing by promoting self-publishing and increasing access.

- Putting library skills to uses outside of the organization is admirably reflected in Florida's Palm Beach County Library System's innovation of embedding librarians in city and county government. Winner of the Urban Libraries Council 2015 "Civic and Community Engagement" initiative, librarians worked as researchers in eight county departments to more effectively serve their community.[20]

These and other examples show how innovative ideas implemented at the right time can change the lives of your clientele for the better and make the library a highly visual, vital, and integral part of the community. It also stresses the need for constant evaluation and assessment with an eye to creating new opportunities as others are no longer relevant.

SCAMPER

Energized? Now it is time to take command of your ideas and capture opportunities you might not even know existed. Let's turn to SCAMPER, a creativity tool that you may use in a group or as an individual, digitally or face to face, in its entirety or as separate parts. The SCAMPER technique was developed by Alex Osborne, who also is credited with inventing the term *brainstorming*. Education administrator and author Bob Eberle created the SCAMPER mnemonic to help children tap into their creativity, and Michael Michalko popularized the process in his books *Thinkertoys* (2006) and *Cracking Creativity* (1998). SCAMPER,[21] an acronym for a set of questions that encourages you to formulate new ideas or modify and expand old ones, is a way to apply structured manipulation to sharpen and polish your ideas. As intrapreneurs have seen for years, everything new stems in one way or another from something that already exists. SCAMPER encourages you to think through your ideas and answer a set of questions. The mnemonic is shown in Figure 5.3. We have

S	**Substitute**: Trial and error ■ What whole or part of a service can you replace with another to create a new opportunity? ■ If you substitute or replace an existing service, what opportunities might appear as a result of that change? ■ Who or what can be substituted in a process? ■ What if I substitute another name for the process? ■ What if I substitute one place for another? ■ What if you changed your attitude or feelings toward the service or product? ■ Key words: replace, change, rename, swap, exchange, alternate, repackage, colorize
C	**Combine**: existing things to see a fresh view ■ What unrelated services can be combined to produce something different? ■ Can we combine services in a different way to produce a new opportunity? ■ Can we combine different talents to improve a service? ■ Can we combine activities? ■ Key words: merge, relate, intermix, mingle, synthesize
A	**Adapt**: what do you already offer that can be adapted to a new use; what have you read about that could be adapted for use in your library? ■ How are we currently dealing with the problem and is it being solved? If so, how can we use aspects of that solution to solve other issues? ■ What practices or processes in use at other libraries can I copy or replicate? ■ What practices in use outside of libraries can be adapted? ■ Who can be adapted to provide a better fit for services? ■ What else is the service or product like? What attributes does it share with another successful endeavor that you can adapt? ■ Key words: adjust, alter, amend, change, copy, emulate, fit into, incorporate, make more flexible, modify, replicate, revise, rework
M	**Increase or Magnify**: what can you expand or make larger? ■ What services can go beyond the library to magnify results? ■ Can you exaggerate part of a service to create brand loyalty? ■ What services can be magnified and service a larger clientele? ■ Can you increase the times a service is offered? Expand physical library hours? Expand online services? ■ How can you add more features? ■ Key words: amplify, augment, boost, expand, increase, multiply, overemphasize, overstress, supplement

Figure 5.3: SCAMPER

P	**Put to Other Uses:** how can we develop current services for different clientele? Different locations? Different times? ■ What services might be more effective in another setting? ■ Can a service that is not working in its current setting be used by people other than those for whom you originally intended it? ■ What can you reuse from another service in the new one? ■ Can a different group of people use it? ■ Can people understand how to use it without instruction? Is it intuitive? What does it imitate? ■ Key words: apply, exercise, manage, manipulate, move, reposition, swap, transfer, transpose
E	**Eliminate or Minify:** what can you take away that would make the service simpler and potentially more valuable? ■ What part of a service is not being used? What whole service can be eliminated based on your clientele's needs? ■ How can I simplify the service? Make it easier to use and understand? ■ Are there any steps in the workflow that we can eliminate? Can it be streamlined to increase value and efficiency? ■ What rules need to be eliminated to make the library more valuable? ■ Can I make it smaller? ■ Keywords: disregard, do away with, eradicate, get rid of, limit, reduce, remove, simplify, underemphasize
R	**Reverse or Rearrange:** move things around to see new patterns and opportunities. ■ How do you change the components to produce a more effective service? ■ How can you change schedules? ■ Can you rearrange the order of processes? Reverse them? ■ Can you swap parts? ■ Will it work backwards? ■ Can I turn it inside out? ■ Keywords: backward, change, flip, invert, move, opposite, rearrange, reorder, reorganize, reposition, reschedule, reshuffle, swap, switch, transpose, turnabout

Figure 5.3: (continued)

added pertinent questions to the process. You can go through the seven areas one after another while asking questions for each area, or you can answer one question in each area and continue sequentially. However you use it, you want to open your mind to new ideas while challenging your assumptions. Beginning with a need or problem, use SCAMPER to generate solutions. When you are finished, select one solution that you want to pursue and move on to the filtering process.

The Distilling Process: Because All Ideas Are Not Created Equal

Let's examine what it takes to filter or distill ideas and to establish if *your* idea is a *good* idea because, let's face it, not all ideas are truly beneficial for your organization. As much as you feel there is a need for your idea, the challenge is to make others understand and embrace it with you. Part of that process involves criticism, and while just about everyone dislikes criticism, even when it is constructive, intrapreneurs must learn to accept it, use it, and thrive on it.

One way to picture this process is to visualize ideas bubbling up fueled by the flames of needs. As the ideas take form and reform, will one idea make it through the brainstorming and facilitation sessions and emerge? Definitely. Will the idea go through permutations along the way? Absolutely. Will some ideas be discarded out of hand? Yes. Will other ideas be put on hold? Count on it. Effective intrapreneurs accept and realize that some form of distilling process holds an integral part of idea generation and acceptance and that the key is to guide the process and convince others to accept and promote the idea.

This distillation process involves assessment, discussion, and feedback along the way. Let's use the analogy of a distillation apparatus or still, perhaps one that produces fine Kentucky Bourbon at the end of the process. You begin with a fire that is a need; it heats up the ideas in the first part of the still, where the mash ferments, boils, expands, and contracts, and finally turns to vapor. Brainstorming produces many ideas, some of which are discarded at this point. Others form vapor and move upward to the top of the pipe. At this point, the idea could still be derailed and filtered out into the *not-now* bucket. Ideas in the not-now bucket are on hold. Perhaps it is not yet the time for this innovation. As other ideas drop off, the distilled liquid coalesces into one idea that pops through and begins to be refined, narrowed, and perfected. It slides down a smaller and smaller pipe. Before it hits the condenser coils, cold water cools it down. The cold water comes from internal and external sources as they assess and question the idea further. If the idea survives, like the liquid, it starts through the torturous route of condenser coils of continuous analysis, a pilot project, and further assessment. When the idea passes these tests, it finally emerges as an innovation ready for implementation. It has made it through the distillation process just like pure and valuable Kentucky Bourbon, as shown in Figure 5.4.

Now that we've looked at the distilling process, let's consider another visual representation: the staircase to success model shown in Figure 5.5. In both methods, after initial idea generation you establish a timeline to give the project a trial, and then accept, modify, or reject it based on feedback.

It all begins with a need and an idea, which is the motivation for the entire process, or the fire that pushes it forward. You have listened

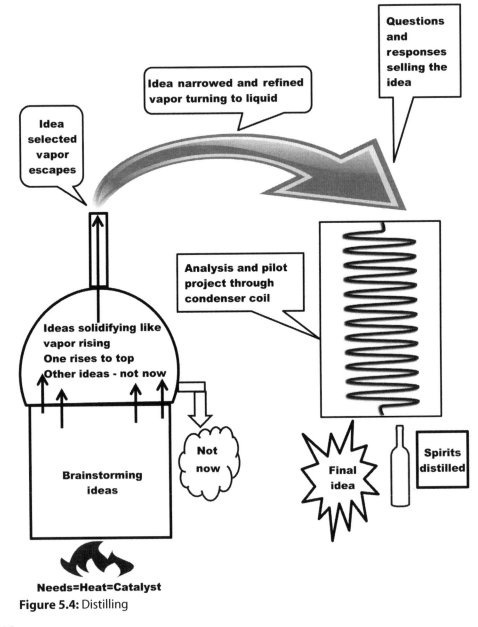

Figure 5.4: Distilling

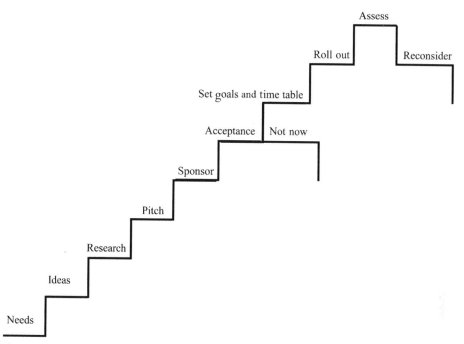

Figure 5.5: Staircase to Success

and asked about a particular service or need for change. The idea firms up. You do the research and generate interest and partnerships. You create a pilot project and solicit customer feedback. You roll out the service while remaining flexible and open to suggestions. Then it is time to assess and fix problems and perhaps even generate a new service or change the one you originally planned. Modifications take place. If the service is a success, continue to evaluate. If it fails, then it's back to the drawing board. On the other hand, one part of the process may be useful, just not the entire thing. For example, you want to change the way a work flow is handled, but it involves moving people from one side of the room to another. Something as small as this could derail an idea. Why? Because those people on one side of the room are by the windows and it took them 10 years to get there. They are not moving without a great deal of complaining and disruption. You decide to make a few modifications to accommodate this reality because remaining inflexible wipes out the entire idea, but being flexible moves your idea forward as well as puts the people who can derail it firmly back on your team. Of course, there will be times when compromise is not an option. In that case, then going forward without full support may be the only option.

What constitutes the most painful part of the distillation process or stair analogy? When your pet project is thrown away. For example, the distillation process reduces many ideas into a smaller number by destroying the weak or unproductive ideas and picking the best one for serving the organization. Are there issues with this process? As with any process, sure there are. Those people who dislike a filtering or distillation process claim that it only produces innovations that are similar to services or ideas that already exist and cannot produce completely innovative results. This is not necessarily true, and ideas that are not wholly innovative continue to fulfill definite needs. Anytime a change fulfills a need you are successful. Another way to look at innovation and change may be found in David Nichols's rocket analogy. Rockets have simple but powerful motors that "turn potent fuel into vast amounts of energy which is directed and built up into maximum thrust—thrust so strong it lifts the entire structure up."[22] Nichols recommends these steps to rocket your way to innovative success.

1. Know your destination: Know where you are going and set clear guidelines. This step ties directly into knowing and understanding your organization's mission and vision statements, as we discussed earlier.

2. Combustion: You have a lot of data, but it is just sitting there. Time to add new insight by looking in different places for input. "If you look in new places in different ways, you are more likely to turn up something potent."[23] Consider SCAMPER and new ways of providing services, collaborations, or products.

3. Set up a drop-dead date for implementation: Agreed-on and set-in-stone deadlines keep everyone on task. You or your colleagues may have great ideas, discuss them to death, and then try to implement a service long after the need has ended. Make sure all members of the innovation team understand the deadline and agree that it is important enough to keep. Many times, of course, budgets or other projects may cause the deadline to slip. It is important to keep up the momentum in spite of obstacles. Turn those obstacles into challenges and meet them head on like Lance Werner did at the Kent District Library.

4. Launch with real rather than test markets: That means less testing and more implementing. Completing a pilot project is not a bad idea, but when you finally take off, make sure you are implementing. Keep the project fresh, timely, and useful.

While Nichol's rocket analogy may not suit every need, it may be a good way to resolve some of the innovation issues plaguing your organization because it promotes a total can-do, go-forward approach.

One excellent example of an innovation that followed the rocket take-off model was the establishment of the Intellectual Property Awareness Center (IPAC) at Steely Library, Northern Kentucky University. It all began with an idea and people willing to ignite the fuel driven by community need. Even though it had to be bootstrapped and done in segments, there was always a clear destination: the need for a one-stop center to educate creators and consumers of intellectual property on the subjects of copyright and fair use, plagiarism, trademarks and patents, and other intellectual properties. The IPAC services this need by providing information resources, workshops, and one-on-one consultations in support of innovative endeavors in the community. It also ties in with institutional and library strategic plans and provides value to the academic and business communities by delivering a service not otherwise addressed by institutions in the geographic area. Implemented in 2011, the IPAC became an official Patent & Trademark Resource Center in 2013.[24]

In a similar vein, Shaun Briley, branch manager at the La Jolla/Riford Library, San Diego Public Library, converted a storage room into the first biotech laboratory in a public library. Called the La Jolla/Riford Branch's Bio Lab, Briley made this innovation a success because he "brainstormed, organized, outfitted, and brought [it] to life with the help of local biohackers and citizen scientists."[25] With state-of-the-art equipment and experienced and degreed volunteers, the lab is receiving national recognition. Briley notes that the lab serves a real need in his community and is reflective of community emphasis: "every community has some focus, something they do in particular, and here it just happens to be biotech."[26]

Define Value and Express the Idea

From the example above, we can see libraries clearly listening to their environment and creating services that provide value in their communities. How do you determine if your idea will provide value for your users? What is value? How can you make services or products even better, less expensive, more mobile, and convenient while personalizing them for your clientele? Value stems from

- demand for your service or product. What does your organization provide that is unique and freely available? Anyone can search the Internet, but what value-added service does a trained professional add? How can you promote the advantages of library purchased databases over information freely available on the Internet?

- users who trust in the ability of your organization to provide accurate and timely service–your reputation, their loyalty. Good will.

- what you do better than your competition. Are your services as easy to use as a smart phone? Adding quality.

- adding new revenue or lowering costs. Monetary value.

Valuable ideas stemming from community and organizational understanding and needs can be generated in different ways, but regardless of how they were generated, you are now ready to express your idea in clear terms. In a nontechnical way, describe the idea in the most succinct way possible while considering the following points:

1. Describe the problem that your idea will fix, enhance, or expand into a new service. Be clear why you want to make a change. This is important because you need to articulate to yourself, your colleagues, your bosses, and the community why a change is necessary.

2. Explain how much time and resources the change will absorb. Set a timeline and explain who will need to do what and when. Be specific and truthful in allotting time and resources to the idea.

3. Define whether this is a fairly quick fix or a long-term radical change. Again, it is a time commitment. How long will it take under normal circumstances?

4. Be honest with yourself and clearly specify how much personal time you are willing to donate to the idea and completion of the change. What are *you* willing to give up? How will this fit into your schedule for work and family?

5. Clarify in simple statements why and how you know that this change is needed at this time. What is your evidence? Word-of-mouth discussions? Client feedback? Staff feedback? Mandates from the organization itself? What does your research show?

6. Where did the idea for change originate? From reading the literature? Suggestions? When and where did you first see the need?

7. Explain what has already been done to address the concern. If nothing, why not? If something has already been done, what were the efforts and why were they unsuccessful? Be quite certain that you

are addressing the right problem at the right time. Is this issue festering with no one willing to resolve it? If so, why? And why you?

8. Does anyone else in your organization or your community care about this issue or see the need for a change? Who is on *your side*?

9. Will you be open to constructive criticism and willing to hand over control of the project to a colleague if asked? Will you become defensive if others offer criticism? Where do you see yourself in this issue? Look at the big picture.

10. What have you already personally done to improve the situation or change it? Is this an entirely new situation that needs attention or one that has lingered? Again, why you, why now?

11. Define the value that such a change will bring to your organization. Consider client satisfaction, streamlined workload, better publicity, and even additional revenue. Why should the organization invest in this idea now? Why not later?

12. Finally, as always, describe how your idea or plan addresses your organization's mission, goals, or objectives. Return to the big picture and clearly explain how, when, why, and where your idea enhances the organization.

One method that can help you further evaluate your ideas and judge value is to conduct a SCORE analysis. The SCORE acronym and its meanings are detailed in the following list:

- *S*trengths: What services, programs, products do you currently provide? What collaborations exist internally and externally? What resources and expertise can your organization bring to the table to provide solutions?

- *C*hallenges: What types of resources does your idea need to succeed? How will you overcome obstacles such as a lack of resources, personnel, time?

- *O*ptions: What opportunities can this idea develop? List the risks involved and consider if the end result is worth the risks. What opportunities will be created for others if this idea is accepted?

- *R*esponses: What happens if your idea is implemented? Are there any unintended consequences? Will you fix one problem only to create another? What if the idea is put on hold or totally rejected? What are the results of that decision?

- *E*ffectiveness: How effective is your idea? Can you measure the effectiveness given clearly outlined parameters? Can you make the most of the resources you have? Is the idea consistent and clear without being overly complicated?

One thing to remember when working through SCORE is that each area needs to be measurable; that is "What's the score?" "What can be measured?" SCORE allows you to measure your idea both before implementation and after and helps you to plug in a continuous improvement module.

Screening, Research, and Feasibility Study: Getting Your Ducks in a Row

After completing an analysis of user feedback and distilling your ideas, it is time to research the idea more fully—certainly a task that librarians excel at—and decide if it truly is feasible for your organization within a given timeframe. You will get your ducks in a row as you assess the organizational impact of your idea and prepare a feasibility study. This is all part of the distilling process—especially important with radical change.

"Wait a minute," you say, "I'm an intrapreneur who is also an employee and I don't have time for this." Actually, you don't have time not to. You are the passionate change agent and thinking is part of your character. Being prepared increases your chance of success and staying on track with a successful implementation timeline. Let's examine the parts of a feasibility study, which include an examination of the idea and the resultant product or service. In looking over the feasibility study points, decide which of them work best for your idea. Completing a feasibility study is a great way to analyze risks and rewards and to quantify your need for resources.

Feasibility Study

Roman numerals represent the main points with pertinent questions beneath each. Go through each question and prepare a document with answers to the questions that pertain to your idea. These answers will be invaluable to you as you proceed further, especially when requesting resources from your organization and justifying a change.

Point I. Describe your idea and how it fits into your organization's goals, objectives, and vision.

- What experience or benefit will the user get from this service or product?

- What do you bring to this idea? What is your background, knowledge, skills, or abilities that will make this service or product a success in your community?
- How does it fit in with other products or services the library already offers?

Point II. Product or service

A. Features and benefits

- What are the unique features and how do these meet your user's needs or requests?
- Are there any competitors who offer this service? If so, who are they and why is yours better?
- Describe the product or service simply and use illustrations to create a visual impact. How does it work? Who will provide it in the library?

B. Features and shortcomings

- List any limitations, including those related to timeliness, reliability, legal or environmental constraints, and learning curves. Honestly assess any disadvantages to your idea.

C. Development stage

- Where is the service or product in terms of development?
- Is it still only an idea or have you talked with others about the opportunities?
- What are the results of your SCORE analysis?
- Did you clearly define your targeted clientele, that is, your target users during the creation of your idea and later when you market it? (See Chapter 9.)

D. Legal restrictions

- Are there any community restrictions? Laws that prohibit the service or product? Internal rules that would have to change? Intellectual property issues? Zoning restrictions?
- Government regulations and requirements? OSHA, IRS, zoning, tax, city, state, and federal laws or restrictions?
- Insurance issues
  - Would the opening of the new service or establishing of the new product impact the library's liability or insurance policies?
  - Consider liability for employees as well as the clientele.

Point III. Community and clientele

- What is the current state of library services nationally and locally? How does your library fit in?

- What kind of competition exists for both library services and your idea?

- Who are your clientele? What demographic information have you researched that explains their characteristics, preferences, values, attitudes?

- How do you know they really want this?

- Although a part of marketing, consider how you will reach the people who will benefit most from this idea?

Point IV. Financial considerations

- Does the service/product have a cost? What is it and how did you set it?

- If no fee is being charged, what is the cost to the library to add the service/product?

Point V. Action plan

- What resources are needed to start and implement the project? Personnel? Money? Space? Equipment? Where will these resources come from?

- List individuals you can consult for help such as mentors or others in or outside of the library who can help you solidify your plan.

- Articles or other information illustrating how similar plans were successful.

Your ducks are in a row. You've isolated and analyzed your idea. You have prepared a document based on the feasibility of your idea. Now it is time to sell and pitch your idea. In the next chapter, we will examine how to sell your idea to your colleagues, board, community, and others. You must be well prepared when you present your idea, and a feasibility study is a good start. As part of the entire idea creation and dissemination process, you also will have enhanced your skills and knowledge by reading pertinent publications, attending free webinars, and taking classes. You have the information and the interest. You are the intrapreneur who will make the change happen.

Notes

1. Peter Cook, "How to Break Down the Barriers and Allow Intrapreneurs to Flourish," *Virgin*, February 3, 2015, http://www.virgin.com/entrepreneur/how-to-break-down-the-barriers-and-allow-intrapreneurs-to-flourish.

2. Dixie Gillaspie, "When Looking for a Solution, Stop Staring at the Problem," *Entrepreneur*, April 24, 2015, http://www.entrepreneur.com/article/245416.

3. This story appears in many different formats. An interesting recounting by K.R. Ravindran, president of Rotary International, appeared in *The Rotarian* (September 2015): 1. Another version appeared in C.R. Jaccard, "Objectives and Philosophy of Public Affairs Education," in *Increasing Understanding of Public Problems and Policies: A Group Study of Four Topics in the Field of Extension Education* (Chicago, IL: Farm Foundation, 1956) http://purl.umn.edu/17341. "A woodsman was once asked, 'What would you do if you had just five minutes to chop down a tree?' He answered, 'I would spend the first two and a half minutes sharpening my axe.' Let us take a few minutes to sharpen our perspective."

4. "Information, we want information" appeared at the beginning of the 1967–1968 television series *The Prisoner* starring Patrick McGoohan.

5. American Library Association, *Librarians and Libraries Can Lead Community Conversations for Change: A Conversation Guide*, http://www.ala.org/transforminglibraries/sites/ala.org.transforminglibraries/files/content/ConversationGuide_final.pdf.

6. Community Branch Manager, E. 38th Street Branch, Indianapolis Public Library and winner in the *Library Journal* 2016 Change Agent category.

7. "Shanika Heyward: Movers & Shakers 2016—Change Agents," *Library Journal* (March 15, 2016), Odds Breaker, http://lj.libraryjournal.com/2016/03/people/movers-shakers-2016/shanika-heyward-movers-shakers-2016-change-agents/.

8. The Indianapolis Public Library, "Library at a Glance," http://www.indypl.org/about/glance/. Vision statement.

9. "Lance Werner: Movers & Shakers 2016—Change Agents," *Library Journal* (March 15, 2016), Back from the Brink, http://lj.libraryjournal.com/2016/03/people/movers-shakers-2016/lance-werner-movers-shakers-2016-change-agents/.

10. Cathy M. Perley and others, "Conducting a User-Centered Information Needs Assessment: The Via Christi Libraries' Experience," *Journal of the Medical Library Association* 95, no. 2 (2007), 173–181, http://www.ncbi.nlm.nih.gov/pmc/articles/PMC1852625/.

11. Library Research Service: Research and Statistics about Libraries Provides Library User Survey Templates for Various Types of Surveys. LRS is associated with the Colorado State Library, which is a unit of the Colorado Department of Education. They "design and conduct library research for library and education professionals, public officials, and the media to inform practices and assessment needs." LRS, 2013, http://www.lrs.org/

library-user-surveys-on-the-web/. OCLC WebJunction, "Library Surveys for Success," Webinar, February 4, 2014; archived, 2016, https://www.webjunction.org/events/webjunction/library-surveys-for-success.html.

12. John A. Ledingham and Stephen D. Bruning, "Ten Tips for Better Focus Groups," *Public Relations Quarterly* 43, no. 4 (Winter 1998/1999): 25.

13. Ibid.

14. Guy Kawasaki, "Ideas Are Easy, Implementation Is Hard," *Forbes*, November 4, 2004, http://www.forbes.com/2004/11/04/cx_gk_1104 artofthestart.html.

15. Kevin DeSouza, *Intrapreneurship: Managing Ideas without Your Organization* (Toronto: University of Toronto Press, 2011), 122.

16. S.R. Winters, "Stretching the Five-Foot Shelf: An Invention That May Reduce the Size of Our Books to a Fraction of Their Present Bulk," *Scientific American* (June 1922): 407.

17. Sharon Almquist, ed. *Distributed Learning and Virtual Librarianship* (Santa Barbara, CA: ABC-CLIO, 2011), 8, 23.

18. Steven Lau, "Library Book-Vending Machines Losing Ground to eBooks," *El Cerrito Patch*, June 29, 2012, http://patch.com/california/elcerrito/library-a-go-go-program-losing-steam-to-e-books.

19. Self-e. 2016, http://self-e.libraryjournal.com/.

20. Urban Libraries Council, Civic and Community Engagement, "Embedded Librarians in County Government," 2015, http://www.urbanlibraries.org/embedded-librarians-in-county-government-innovation-1192.php?page_id=420.

21. The questions used in the SCAMPER process were developed by Alex Osborne, who is credited with creating the term *brainstorming*. Education administrator and author Bob Eberle created the SCAMPER mnemonic to help children tap into their creativity. Michael Michalko popularized the process in his books *Thinkertoys* (2006) and *Cracking Creativity* (1998). Bill Jarrard, "The History of S.C.A.M.P.E.R," *Mindwerx International*, http://www.mindwerx.com/mind-tools/5762/history-s-c-m-p-e-r.

22. David Nichols, Why Innovation Funnels Don't Work and Why Rockets Do," *Market Leader* (Autumn 2007): 26–31, http://thebrandgym.com/downloads/bgym%20Market%20Leader%20Innovation%20Rocket%20article%20-%20Sept%2007.pdf.

23. Ibid., 30.

24. Northern Kentucky University, "Intellectual Property Awareness Center," 2016, http://ipac.nku.edu/. John Schlipp, phone call with Sharon Almquist, March 31, 2016. Schlipp is the associate professor and intellectual property librarian at Steely Library, Northern Kentucky University, and formerly the patent and trademark librarian at the Cincinnati and Hamilton Company Public Library.

25. "Shaun Briley: Movers & Shakers 2016—Innovators," *Library Journal* (March 15, 2016), Toward Bioliteracy, http://lj.libraryjournal.com/2016/03/people/movers-shakers-2016/shaun-briley-movers-shakers-2016-innovators/.

26. Roxana Popescu, "The Latest DIY Biotech Hot Spot? The Local Library," *Washington Post*, October 20, 2015, http://www.washingtonpost.com.

CHAPTER 6

Pitching Your Idea and Getting Others to Join

A status quo attitude will render an organization ineffective and condemn it to obsolescence and lack of support.

—Library and Information Center Management

Pitching isn't only useful for raising money—it's an essential tool for reaching agreement on any subject. Agreement can yield many outcomes: management buy-in for developing a product or service, securing a partnership, recruiting an employee, or securing an investment.

—Guy Kawaski, Art of the Start[2]

"'The time has come,' the Walrus said, 'to talk of many things: Of shoes—and ships—and sealing-wax—Of cabbages—and kings— And why the sea is boiling hot—And whether pigs have wings.'"[3] Like Lewis Carroll's walrus, it is time to address several crucial ways to encourage the successful acceptance of your idea, such as how to pitch your idea and get support and buy-in from your organization; how to deliver an effective elevator speech and presentation; how to handle acceptance and rejection; how to create a working innovator's plan; and how to understand and integrate budget considerations into your proposal. Remember that many different people or stakeholders make up your organization: the end users of your idea, people who use the library as well as fellow employees.

Simply put, it is time to campaign for your idea and select the appropriate audience for your promotion. It is time to sell your idea to those who may be eager to support a change or to those who may be risk averse. In either case, the challenge you face is to select, then impress, inspire, and convince your audience even if you are not sure how, or whether, the group will accept your idea. Your goal is to create enthusiasm, not aversion; to soothe and appeal to risk-averse mentalities; and to never lose sight of your primary objective: your plan for innovation.

Libraries are dynamic organizations, but as a rule, innovative ideas do not fit effortlessly within existing organizations. Instead, as discussed in other chapters, change agents must understand the organization, its goals and objectives, strategic plans, vision and mission, internal and external clientele, and the community it serves. They need to know the current state of the organization, know the internal and external forces that can affect decisions, understand budgeting and personnel concerns, and be able to see the big picture. In other words, be prepared to think like a manager. With that accomplished, the intrapreneur may then seek out a sponsor, a person who has the authority to run interference for the intrapreneur and assign resources and secure permissions. The intrapreneur then is free to build his advocate base by selling the idea to the right people at the right time. One effective method for gaining support is the elevator speech. Once you capture your listener's interest with a short but passionate appeal, you can then arrange a time to talk at length.

Writing and Delivering the Elevator Speech

You are a busy person. So are your supervisors and peers. Why waste their time as well as your own with long-winded explanations that detail, with excessive jargon, every single aspect of your idea? Leave those details for the innovator's plan—also known as a business plan. Begin by synthesizing your idea into a 30–60-second (100–250 words or fewer) explanation or advertisement. It is challenging to synthesize a whole plan into that short timeframe, but ultimately gratifying. It allows you to express the most important reason for your idea while you seek to persuade others to not only listen, but invest their time and energy. You want to spark others' interest in your project. Never assume that because the idea is of maximum interest to you, it will also be so for others. An effective elevator speech makes the listener ask, "Tell me more about this idea" or "Let's get together over coffee tomorrow because I want to know more."

Your elevator speech must be brief and to the point because research indicates that many listeners lose interest after 30 seconds. Some studies even show that the average human has a shorter attention span than the average goldfish: humans eight seconds, goldfish nine seconds.[4] TV or radio commercials average 30 seconds, which is also the average length of an elevator ride. You have a captive audience in an elevator, but only for a short period of time: about the amount of open time your supervisor might have on a busy day. Although some experts might allow up to a two-minute speech, most agree that short, passionate, cogent, and interesting pitches are the best. Remember, an elevator speech works to generate initial interest and create advocates for your idea at both the initial phase of acceptance and later when you promote and celebrate the idea.

Take the time to carefully craft your speech to garner support from people in your organization. While you should change the pitch to reflect the interests of your audience, having your ideas organized can help you to get them across more effectively. Here are a few tips to help you craft an effective elevator speech:

- Begin with a hook—what is most memorable about the idea? "Our faculty isn't using our library effectively." "Let's create a unique opportunity for our youngest library users."

- Explain in one sentence what you hope to accomplish through your innovation and how it brings value to the organization. How will your innovation make people happy? "Embedding a librarian in several departments will increase faculty interest in our services." "Providing off-site access to our gerontology database will let our patrons work from home."

- State why it is imperative that the innovation go forward now. Your needs assessment or feasibility study suggested that faculty do not feel that they have time to come to the library. How to create urgency that this must be fixed right now? "Faculty will lose interest in our services if we cannot provide a librarian to attend their faculty meetings!"

- State why you need that individual's help by highlighting her outstanding characteristics. Or state that it can only be done with the help of the entire organization. "Your assigning faculty members to departments will show that the library is an integral part of the campus." "Our library can be at the forefront of fighting the terrible heroin addiction in our community."

- Be passionate, but not overbearing. Use your body language to invoke enthusiasm, but be careful to appear non-threatening. "We need to take advantage of this opportunity before prices go up!"

- Practice in front of a mirror or webcam. Memorize your speech, but keep the presentation fresh. Think of alternative hooks that you can use to best appeal to your audience.

- Listen to the feedback people give you. Don't be so in love with your idea that you cannot tolerate any constructive suggestions. Do not take "not now" as an insult if you approach someone who is busy. Be polite and ask when would be a good time to discuss a crucial issue, such as during a coffee break. Take the time to come to someone's office at his convenience.

Use the worksheet (see Figure 6.1) to improve your speech and help you work out the kinks. Ask a colleague to listen and critique your

Points to Address	Suggestions
If you do not know your listener (audience) personally, introduce yourself and your organization.	Hello, my name is [name] and I'm from the library.
	Mr. Mayor, I'm [name] from the library.
If you do know your listener, you can still introduce yourself and, if your organization is large, your department.	Hi, I'm [name] from the cataloging department.
	I'm from our newly remodeled School Library Learning Commons.
Hook—Give your audience a reason to listen to you ■ question ■ observation ■ need ■ positive can do "we" not "I"	Have you seen the large number of students coming in after school?
	Let's create that new makerspace with a grant for a 3-D printer!
	Changing that cataloging procedure can make us 100% more efficient and save time!
	We'd like you to come see the difference in what happens there.
	Remember the time we didn't . . .
	We can make a difference by. . . .
	Did you know that . . .
	We just discovered . . .

Figure 6.1: Elevator Speech Worksheet

What is innovation? Begin by writing about it in different ways. Just throw out words and ideas. Use short phrases rather than full sentences. Brainstorm. Edit, think, repeat.	Generates interest for after-school students Allows more online access Expands hours on Saturday Teachers and students put their lessons into real world situations. Brings in new events Grants Brings opportunities for partnerships
What is your goal? ■ to gain support for your innovation ■ to add value to your library ■ to serve the underserved in the community ■ to partner with outside sources to create a new service ■ obtain a grant	Need at least $5,000 for equipment Need support from the reference department Need help writing a grant proposal Need flex time to complete the innovative plan
Write 10–20 action statements that explain how you will complete the project if given support	■ with the money we will purchase ■ with extra time we can plan ■ sharing duties will allow us to
Pick out the most informative and interesting aspects. Don't dwell on specific details at this point, save that for your innovation plan. Hook with vivid words and a clear picture.	■ we can create the makerspace ■ we can support the children's summer reading program ■ we can purchase a bookmobile ■ we can provide breakfast for the children of working parents in the summer when school is not in session Collaborating teachers add art and music to the study of other countries in the world.
Explain the payoff: what will the service provide to the community?	Our project has the potential to promote a significant gain in reading readiness for pre-K children.
Ask for help. Ask for a meeting to further discuss the idea. Create a card or brief handout with your contact information and key points of your speech. Ask if you can send your listener more information.	Can you help? Could we meet at your convenience? May I send you more information? Here's a flyer with more information and the website. When would you be available for a visit?

Figure 6.1: (continued)

pitch; then start pitching to those you feel are sympathetic. As the idea snowballs, others may also take up the elevator speech in support of your idea. In smaller libraries, getting into the community and being prepared to promote your idea, and your library, at a moment's notice can enhance your chances of getting support when you most need it and least expect it.

Thirty seconds is not enough time, you argue. For many people, perhaps not, but being able to arrange your thoughts so that you can present them clearly in a short timeframe helps you to pitch even more effectively after you have captured your audience. On the other hand, what things can derail your efforts at pitching in that short a timeframe? There are several:

- Not pitching to the correct audience because you didn't do your homework and do not fully understand the people you are trying to get on board.

- Being overly eager and breathlessly jumping into a conversation.

- Not reading your audience's body language; that is, is she really interested right now?

- Becoming defensive if the person is not interested.

- Becoming a victim because "they didn't get it!" It is your job to see that they do get the message because you are patient and professional.

- Above all remember: it's not all about *you*! "Stay out of your problems. Stay in their solutions."[5] In other words, focus on the idea and the results. How are you helping others? Are you asking others to move outside of their comfort zones?

Getting a Sponsor: Turning the Elevator Speech into a Pitch

If you are going to turn your promotional elevator speech into a full pitch you may have to consider getting someone in authority, either within or outside of your organization, or both, to assist you with getting the idea accepted and implemented. Decide what format you will use for your pitch and then to take it to the next step.

If you are going to be successful in generating interest both within and outside of your library and are motivated, positive, and focused, you need to sell the idea to someone in the organization who can help you to realize your goals. This may be your supervisor, the library board, a dean, or director, but it is someone who has the authority to assist you with the change. Begin by working with your supervisor first to allow him to buy into your plan. Provide the information your supervisor will need to make an informed decision. For example, your supervisor may ask: how will you handle the extra work? If asked this question, you will need to reassure him that your project won't distract you from work already assigned. Be careful how you answer. If you appear to be too busy, your supervisor may want you to put off the innovation. If you give the impression of excess hours in a day, the boss may wonder why you did not suggest this sooner or whether you have been assigned enough work to keep you busy! Explain how the innovation fits into your current workload and, if necessary, show how you will put in extra hours to make it happen because "employees who are passionate about the company, and skilled enough to implement their passion, are an invaluable asset, and will be far more useful to a company than those who simply show up to work to complete the bare minimum of what's required of them."[6]

Another must is to put yourself in your boss's shoes because everyone has to justify changes to someone. Clearly articulate the benefits that come from your proposal. Seek to create a win-win environment for everyone involved. Susan Inouye, an executive coach, recommends that if "we let go of our egos and look towards our boss as a mentor in the development and implementation of our idea and are willing to share the credit with them, the more invested they become. We must remember that their contributions are necessary to get it done."[7]

What if the boss says "no"?

Try to find out if this is "no" at this time or a final "no." Be clear about the meaning of "no." Ask for feedback and consider the following:

- Is it the wrong time?
- Did you fail to make a case for needed additional resources?
- Did you request personnel from another project that has priority?
- Did you approach your boss in a confrontationist manner because you are so passionate about your idea?

With the answers to these questions you will know whether to revise and return or give up the project altogether.

As part of the pitching process, some authors suggest that in order to sell your ideas internally, one format you might consider is to create a video with colleagues and/or clientele. Interview and create a video with people who support the idea and learn how its adoption will benefit them. The video shows your take-charge attitude and ability to get things accomplished. You have taken your time and effort to make a change.[8] Above all, be respectful of others' time and edit the video to a reasonable length—no more than three minutes. Use the video to make your idea pop and generate excitement for a change.

When you are ready to take your pitch outside of the organization, usually with your supervisor's blessing, consider asking to be invited to a meeting of the local Rotary Club, Kiwanis group, school board, PTA, Lions Club, or homeschool group. The easiest way to be invited to speak in your local community is to be an active member of your community and an advocate for your library. Join groups and attend meetings and let people know who you are and why you are there. You have already been using your elevator speech at every opportunity to promote your idea and the library. Encourage leaders in these groups to invite you for a longer presentation.

To develop a longer, and perhaps more formal, presentation, begin by working through a series of questions and providing answers that will serve as the outline for the presentation. Use a feasibility study to help flesh out the outline. Consider these key points.

- What situation encouraged you to formulate the idea? What is your evidence for this conclusion? Did you use feedback from surveys, focus groups, observations?

- Define clearly why a situation needs to be changed or the need is important. What is your vision? How does it tie in with your organization's vision? With community initiatives?

- What have you or your organization already done to alleviate the situation?

- Why is your idea timely? Why now and not later? How soon must the issue be solved?

- What are the proposed results of adopting your solution? What are the alternatives if it is not adopted?

- What unforeseen issues might arise if your proposal is put into place?

- Who needs to be involved internally or externally?

- Money: What grants or community initiatives can support the project? Is any additional funding needed? Are there grant writers in your organization? Have you studied the grants process and sources? How have you reached out to those in your community who can help?

- Your time? It is difficult to be both intrapreneur and employee especially given that the organization pays you for being an employee. Most small libraries cannot afford to bankroll exclusive change agents. How will you convince your audience that you and your colleagues can handle the extra work? Know the organization you are addressing, so that they look favorably upon your wish to be an active player in their goals and an effective change agent. You are not only selling your idea, you are selling trust in yourself as a person who can do it! Prove to your audience that you can handle the responsibility.

- Remain positive at all times even when the questions are difficult to address. If you don't know an answer, make it clear that you will find a solution and are willing to address it at a later date in whatever form of response best suits the asker.

Setting Up the Pitch Presentation

How many of us have sat through very long and very boring presentations? In trying to win support and create ambassadors for your idea, don't fall into the trap of making a boring presentation. If you do choose to make your pitch presentation using PowerPoint, PREZI, or Google Slides,[9] consider the following. Guy Kawasaki's advice is 10 slides, 20 minutes, 30-point font for the text. Use pictures, bullets, and diagrams to make your point, and try to incorporate some *action* on your slides so that it is not a ho-hum flat text-only slide, one after another. You want to stimulate interest and concentrate on essentials, but you want to keep your audience interested. Keep some slides in reserve with greater details so that if asked you have them ready to answer with statistics. Many audiences love details, but you do not want to get bogged down in implementation details at this point. Even if your potential audience gives you an hour, aim for 20 minutes to leave room for discussion and questions.[10] The question and answer section is as important as the pitch. Use the checklist worksheet in Figure 6.2 to polish your presentation.

Slide Content	Your Content
Slide 1 Title of Project Your name and department Your vision statement for the project	
Slide 2 State the problem and describe why it is an issue now—emphasize the opportunity	
Slide 3 Explain your solution and how it will support the library's mission	
Slide 4 Explain how you came to the solution: surveys, needs analysis, observations	
Slide 5 Describe what has already been done. (Nothing?) Why?	
Slide 6 What resources you need make it happen Sources of money Be specific in your needs, yet think big	
Slide 7 How the solution will affect workloads, resources, physical space	
Slide 8 Outcomes—how the solution will add value to the organization Timeline	
Slide 9 Comments from clientele or peers supporting your proposition Include short video clip of interviews Show value	
Slide 10 Questions?	

Figure 6.2: The Pitch: Slide Presentation Checklist

Acceptance and Rejection

What if the audience says "no"? Sometimes you have to be patient. Evaluate your plan and pitch and consider these actions:

- Ask for feedback, preferably formally in writing or informally outside of the organization or group. Suggest meeting individually with the people involved. Ask if there are alternatives.

- Always consider: is it the wrong time?

- What frustrations can be resolved between you and the audience? Did they consider your idea too radical and disruptive? Too little a change?

- Did you fail to offer any alternatives for financing the project? Grants? Partnerships in the community? Intrapreneur expert Gifford Pinchot notes: "The intrapreneurial warrior gets people involved before asking them for anything costly."[11]

- Do you need to reframe your approach? Pinchot defined reframing as "creating a new way of looking at a situation to move a person from negative states like anger, worthlessness, or defensiveness toward ways of seeing the situation that give energy, life, productivity and affection."[12]

- Did your proposal scare people? Are you going to drag them out of their comfort zones?

Don't feel rejected and definitely don't get angry; ask for advice. Is there anything we can do differently to make it work? What did I fail to include? Try to get buy-in as people add their ideas to yours. Thank those giving positive, and even negative, feedback. "Thank you for that suggestion. I can see how that will make the solution even better." For those individuals who set themselves up as an enemy and may provide personal, and in some cases unwarranted, criticism, you can sometimes turn them into advocates by directing their criticism into a form of support.

Critic:	"I just think you are going way beyond your abilities and fail to understand where this organization should be going."
Intrapreneur:	"Perhaps you are right about my abilities, but if you were to help out I believe we can make this a truly successful intraprise."
Critic:	"Well, I may be able to help, but it's just going to so much time and effort."
Intrapreneur:	"If we all work together and continue to support our library's goals, we can really make effective change. When would you like to meet to discuss this?"

Embracing Acceptance

The applause at the end of your presentation is thunderous. Take a few moments to bask in a job well done, but only a few minutes because now the real work begins. It is time to establish a timeframe for a pilot test so you can develop a full *innovator's plan* that will pave the way for implementation of your accepted idea. This small-scale trial or pilot test of the project is a great way to work out the possible glitches before developing your innovation plan. Working with a small group and learning of any possible problems so you can fix them before you inadvertently build a potential problem into the full-scale plan is a smart move. This is especially true with radical projects that may involve changes in personnel or key programs. Based on feedback from the smaller group, you could revise the project plans, if needed. Some parts of it might have to be removed, while other processes may have to be added. This gives you useful results quickly and with a minimum of personnel or monetary expenditure. It strengthens your project and helps to create value.

On the other hand, if the project is seriously flawed, the pilot test will point out these challenges. This may mean that it is not the right project for your clientele right now. Create your test group from a diverse group while considering who will make the best test group. You may want to invite some wild cards, people who don't fit the established norm, to participate in the test especially if you are planning radical change. Schedule some time to meet with your test group, either individually or in groups. Listen to what they have to say, and write up a document describing the pros and cons of your idea. Chances are you will receive even more ideas for innovation as a result. The pilot test will also allow you to assemble a team that can use hard data to move a project forward.

With pilot test results and feedback, you are ready to start your innovator's plan.

The Innovator's Plan

The innovator's plan is loosely based on the type of business plan entrepreneurs use to build legitimacy for their companies. Katz and Green[13] explain the classic business plan with the major characteristics of a company, such as product or service, the overall industry and market it is working in, how it will operate, and financial considerations detailing how it will make money. A business plan also provides internal understanding for those involved in the business; it explains how the business operates and allows entrepreneurs to organize their thoughts regarding the business and its purpose and internal operations. Katz and Green emphasize that the plan must explain how the business will function. Like the business plan, the innovator's plan explains the proposed product or service, the clientele who will be served, and how it will operate. Of course, rather than talking about how the project will make money, the innovator's plan discusses sustainability of the innovation since libraries are generally not profit-making concerns.[14] Depending on the innovation, the change agent may choose to follow a strict plan or adapt the general plan to meet her needs.

The innovator's plan is built on the pitch, which was in turn built on client feedback and idea generation. If your pitch was successful, your innovator's plan is already partially written. Incorporate the feedback from the pitch into the plan, assemble and work with your team, and pave the way for a successful implementation.

One of the most important parts of the plan is the executive summary. Many of those people interested in your project will only read the executive summary. How long should it be? Ideally between four paragraphs to two pages. Here is where you address the key points of the innovation: cogent description of the problem, the solution, the resources needed to solve it, the value created for the organization.

Other key points of the innovator's plan include support for the solution; resources needed and the financial aspects, such as what it will

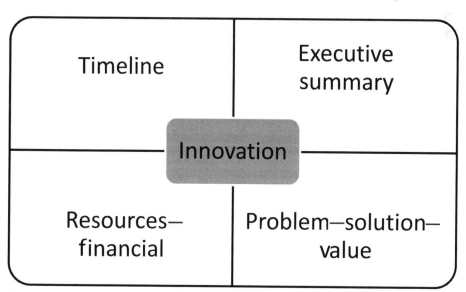

Figure 6.3: Key Points of the Innovator's Plan

cost in terms of money and personnel; and timeline for implementation and review. It is generally recommended that one person write the draft of the plan. Then you can use it to work with your team, which you will assemble, as detailed in the next chapter. Working as a team, your evaluation of the plan forces cooperation and debate. The plan may bring to light details left out of the pilot project as well as new ways to perform some of the tasks. As Guy Kawasaki notes, "the document itself is not nearly as important as the process that leads to the document. Even if you aren't trying to raise money, you should write one anyway."[15] Figure 6.3 illustrates key components of the plan.

Funding the Plan

At this point, you will consider how you will fund your plan. Realize that all plans require some level of resources to put them into operation. While there may be no direct financial investment, there will be personnel costs. (Staff time is worth money, and if someone is working on your project, even if it is only you, that person is not available to work on other projects or to provide ongoing services). In addition, there are *opportunity* costs. That is, by doing your project, other projects or operations (opportunities) may be postponed or permanently cancelled.

The realization that costs are involved in the implementation of any plan helps you to better communicate with your supervisor to request resources that will be needed. Going forward with a request for permission stating that your plan "won't cost anything" will suggest to administrators a certain level of naïveté, which will certainly damage your credibility. If you bring forward a plan which takes into account the time and labor cost (including benefits) that will be required to operationalize your plan, you will have much more credibility with your boss and upper administration and stand a better chance for getting permission to proceed. In terms of direct costs, depending on the size of the project, the state of your organization's budget, and competing needs, there are multiple ways in which the project could be funded.

Securing Necessary Resources from Your Organization

When you request resources from your organization, much will depend on the level of credibility that you have earned from your administration, which heavily depends on your past interactions. Does the administration know you for your honest assessments in previous requests for resources? Are you honest in your assessments of consequences for not carrying out a proposed change? With limited resources and competing needs, it is critical that you have a strong bond of trust in place when you make your request.

If the project requires only reassignment of personnel, permission might be readily given. If your project will require actual budget allocation, the request might need to be added to the library's financial plan. Your boss may need to go to a higher level to request support. In this case, give your administration as much lead time as possible.

In many library situations, it is anticipated that librarians in academic, public, and school libraries should seek outside funding for those projects that are already not in the general budget if the project is for the near-term future. This often means that you must seek outside funding and the first place to look is grant funding.

Outside Funding Sources

Grant funding can be tapped to finance innovation projects when your project fits the granting agency guidelines. Grants are available from private foundations and from all levels of government. These are very competitive and not always difficult to locate.

State libraries often offer grants to public libraries through state funding projects and through their reallocation of Library Services and Technology Act (LSTA) funds. Whether those funds are available for academic or school libraries depends upon the state plan for LSTA.

While the process of grant seeking is beyond the scope of this book, you may find help in a book by Hall-Ellis et al.: *Librarian's Handbook for Seeking, Writing, and Managing Grants*:

> In addition to capitalizing on collective skill, cooperation and teamwork foster creativity and encourage accountability among team members. With many projects to choose from, funding agencies are especially responsive to those that address documented needs in novel and creative ways.[16]

You may also seek out the help of a grant professional in your community. If it is to be a cooperative venture with another type of library, coordinate between grant offices. Those working in public libraries may find that their supporting municipal or county government has a grants professional on its payroll. Larger school districts or regional centers such as county offices also may have someone to help with grants, as do colleges and universities. The grants professional will bring specialized knowledge and experience to the process of grant seeking, facilitate connections with people in the granting agencies, and equally as important, contribute experience in managing grant funds and fulfilling reporting requirements.

Someone in authority in your organization will have to sign off on your application to indicate that the organization supports it. This ensures that the institution is aware of any obligations it may need to provide, such as facilities needed to carry out the project or in-kind contributions for a matching grant as well as overhead charges.

Other Support for Projects

Another way to pay for innovation is by getting someone from outside of the organization to pay for it. The intrapreneur generally must tread carefully in this area since donors are jealously guarded both by library leaders and by people in the parent organization. Always make sure that you contact, get permission, and work with your administration when pursuing this approach.

Will your project result in benefits for the greater community? Are you doing something that will impact P-12 education, involving early childhood reading/learning readiness, creating a service that will connect people with or preserve their heritage? There is a constituency or a cause for each of these examples, and you might well find it easier to connect a donor with this type of special project than many of the day-to-day projects that we see in our libraries.

Most recently, intrapreneurs are beginning to turn to crowd funding to support innovation. Again, you must have a project with which people can quickly develop an emotional connection. Like the crowd funding used by entrepreneurs to fund profit-making concerns, in the non-profit sector, the technique allows multiple small investors to pool their money to support a worthwhile and compelling project. Again, check with your institution or organization to see if a crowd-funding mechanism is already in place.

Now that you have a viable project, it is time to assemble your team and determine your place in it. Even if you did much of the preliminary alone work, you still need a team of supportive individuals who share your vision and will work together to make meaningful change in your organization.

Notes

1. Barbara B. Moran, Robert D. Stueart, and Claudia J. Morner, *Library and Information Center Management*, 8th ed. (Santa Barbara, CA: Libraries Unlimited, 2013), 60.
2. Guy Kawasaki, *The Art of the Start: The Time-Tested, Battle-Hardened Guide for Anyone Starting Anything* (New York: Portfolio, 2004), 44.
3. Lewis Carroll, "The Walrus and the Carpenter," in *Through the Looking-Glass and What Alice Found There* (Rathway, NJ: The Mershon Co., 1900), 66.
4. Microsoft Canada, *Attention Spans-Consumer Insights* (Spring 2015). 6.
5. Sam Harrison, *Idea Selling: Successfully Pitch Your Creative Ideas to Bosses, Clients and Other Decision-Makers* (Cincinnati, OH: HOW Books, 2010), 2.
6. Saksham Kapoor, "Why Going Corporate Doesn't Mean Going Rogue: The Rise of Intrapreneurship," *Startup 88*, January 17, 2015, http://startup88.com/opinion/2015/01/17/going-corporate-doesnt-mean-going-rogue-rise-intrapreneurship/13801.
7. Kathryn Tuggle, "5 Steps to Selling an Idea to Your Boss," *The Street*, October 2, 2013, http://www.thestreet.com/story/12055474/1/5-steps-to-selling-an-idea-to-your-boss.html.
8. Alexandra Levit, *They Don't Teach Corporate in College: A Twenty-Something's Guide to the Business World*, 3rd ed. (Pompton Plains, NY: Career Press, 2014), 100–1.
9. Prezi, https://prezi.com/; Google Slides, https://www.google.com/slides/about/.
10. Kawasaki, *The Art of the Start*, 48–50.
11. Gifford Pinchot, "Getting the Resources You Need: The Way of the Intrapreneurial Warrior," *The Pinchot Perspective*, March 29, 2013, http://www.pinchot.com/2013/03/getting-the-resources-you-need-the-way-of-the-intrapreneurial-warrior.html.
12. Ibid.
13. Jerome A. Katz and Richard P. Green II, *Entrepreneurial Small Business*, 4th ed. (New York: McGraw-Hill, 2014), 216.
14. Ibid.
15. Kawasaki, *The Art of the Start*, 68.
16. Sylvia D. Hall-Ellis et al., *Librarian's Handbook for Seeking, Writing, and Managing Grants* (Santa Barbara, CA: Libraries Unlimited, 2011), xv.

CHAPTER 7

An Innovation Team and Your Place in It

As a change agent, you can never change the world on your own. Yes, you can have ideas and insights as an individual. But the *doing*, that's the one thing you have to engage in together.

— Anis Bedda, cofounder, Intrapreneurship Conference[1]

Intrapreneurship is not a one-person show or a one-team activity. You need a community approach to get the concept off the ground and to hold it together. . . . The organization must drive the process and take ownership of it.

— Kevin DeSouza[2]

Let's examine why forming a team is so necessary to the intrapreneurial process. To begin with, why should you consider a team? Aren't all intrapreneurs solo revolutionaries working on their own? Hardly. Effective intrapreneurs see a need, design a solution, pitch their idea, and take the steps necessary to secure institutional support. After receiving the green light to proceed with the project, they seek out others who can help create a successful organizational improvement or innovation. Intrapreneurs need people who will not only buy into the idea, but commit their time and resources as well. As a team, these employees work together within an intrapreneurial environment with the endorsement of the administration to make the idea a worthwhile reality. Simply put, an innovation team is one whose members elevate the project over their own personal interests, loyally and enthusiastically support and promote it, and consider each member of the team to be equally accountable for completing his assigned tasks in support of the team's goals. In taking this can-do attitude, the team's accomplishments become more than a sum of its individual parts.

But how can you ensure that the intrapreneurial team will work together successfully? In this chapter, we'll examine a number of ways to help make this happen. Forming a team is not an easy task and understanding diverse personalities is a key component to any team's success. Consider the following guidelines that help to establish the foundation on which to build.

1. Setting up a team for success: Why is formal, but flexible, necessary? How many people should constitute the innovation team?

2. Choosing team members: Who should select them? What characteristics are desirable?

3. Assigning roles and responsibilities: Who does what on the team? To whom does the team report?

4. Managing the team: What reports and documentation are required? How do you set and commend milestones? How are changes made? Setting guidelines and timetables. Establish priorities and promote understanding of the innovator's plan. Review time required for the project in view of organizational priorities and individual assignments.

5. Rewards and incentives: Encourage the team and provide rewards for milestones and completion.

Setting Up a Team for Success

> Keep in mind, these highly autonomous "teams of 10" needed to check in every two to four weeks to show progress. They had support. They had to work within a system. They had accountability. And that's the secret of innovative teams: this ability to have autonomy, to have freedom, but within a strong, well-defined support system and with clear accountability.
> —*Forbes* magazine publisher Rich Karlgaard, author of *The Soft Edge: Where Great Companies Find Lasting Success*[3]

Sometimes, we as innovators consider formal procedures, rules, and regulations aggravating and feel that they are unnecessary. But, if we look at these functions as supports rather than obstacles, a change agent can use them to her advantage. To that end, consider the pros and cons of formal versus informal teams.

There are several negatives inherent in an informal team. Informal teams frequently suffer from a lack of authority or urgency or both. The team members and the process may take second place to other projects deemed more important in the eyes of both the employees and their supervisors. If the team meets informally outside of working hours, people are not always willing, or able, to volunteer their time in addition to their normal work load.[4] When a team is not formalized, members may spend more time arguing over who should do what rather than getting work done. Team size may fluctuate, with people leaving when they become overwhelmed or others sabotaging the project because they weren't asked or did not approve of the project's goals. Ultimately, the project may simply die from an unintentional lack of commitment.

On the other hand, a formal team, acknowledged and supported by the organization, lends credibility to the project and to the team members assigned to it. The team can function somewhat autonomously and create its own internal structure even while it supports the goals of the organization. That said, formally created teams should still remain flexible so that they can move quickly. Many experts equate intrapreneurial teams with entrepreneurial startups, those enterprises that move quickly to address a new issue or design a new product.

This leads us to ask: how many people should make up the innovation team? Perhaps the best answer is the fewer the better. Ideally, team size should total between 5 and 12 people. To highlight this recommendation, Amazon CEO Jeff Bezos is credited with coining the *two pizza rule*: meaning that if you cannot feed your team with just two pizzas, the team has too many people. [5] Smaller teams allow members to communicate more efficiently. Fewer people allow for greater flexibility in scheduling times to meet and facilitate getting permission to put other projects aside for the duration of the innovative endeavor since fewer areas will be impacted. Fewer people ought to allow for everyone to have an equal voice and keep team members motivated.

Choosing Team Members

Who should select the members of the innovation team? Who is the person ultimately responsible for the success of the team? Is it the intrapreneur, an administrator, or someone else with either technical or managerial expertise? The answer to these questions depends upon the project itself and its needs as well as its end goal. If adding an individual to your team requires administrative approval, your supervisor may need to select the team and assign a chair, which may—or may not—be you, the intrapreneur. The team reports to the chair that is responsible for the team's success and for any liaison activities between the team and administration. In addition, if a team member does not work out, then the chair replaces him with another person or chooses to not replace that member.

Who should be on the team? The team must be comprised of people who

- are able to work well together;
- are willing to accept, embrace, and promote change in a collegial way;
- consistently maintain a positive attitude toward the organization;
- are ethical and embrace the values of respect and integrity;
- bring pertinent skills and abilities to the project.

The team must share the vision that the intrapreneur outlined in the innovator's plan. Putting someone on the team as a *devil's advocate*, that is, one who openly rejects the idea, will only cause unnecessary conflict. As Robert B. Tucker cogently suggests, "refuse to fill your team with neurotics, narcissists, and loafers even if they are 'talented.' They will drag you down every time. Go after what the late Steve Jobs called 'A Players,' for 'they can run circles around a giant team of B and C players.'"[6] Selectively picking the right people for the team saves the organization time and resources—and the change agent much frustration.

To help in the selection process, many teams apply the BOSI approach developed by Joe Abraham. The BOSI challenge invites change agents to their Web site for a free assessment that will help determine their personal BOSI intrapreneurial DNA as well as that of their team members.[7] Once there, you may choose the *employee* or other assessments. BOSI has the potential to categorize each team member by her general type or types. Abraham's overall BOSI types detail the following categories:

- B for builder
- O for opportunist
- S for specialist
- I for innovator

Using Abraham's outline, you can examine ways to build an effective innovation team. Builders like to build. They are frequently the *idea hamsters* (a serial idea generator) of a group. They are passionate and driven. They can be inconsiderate of others, but not overly so. They assume that everyone around them shares their passion and commitment and are upset when they find that is not the case. The opportunist is usually the intrapreneur who wants to get the project up and running quickly and is always optimistic of its success and value. Specialists are analytical, such as accountants or catalogers. Innovators are the mad scientist librarians of the group. They love what they do but are not necessarily oriented to making the innovation a success. They just love the idea and want to help others no matter what. Sometimes, they are not very practical.

Figure 7.1 illustrates some key innovation team member characteristics.

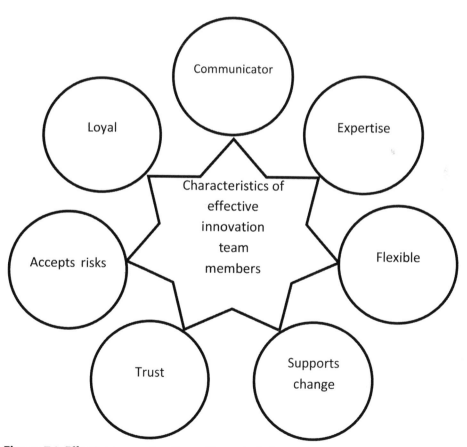

Figure 7.1: Effective Innovation Team Characteristics

Even if you are a mad scientist librarian, you should make a case for selecting the members of the innovation team. Consult with your administration and/or supervisor, that person who approved your idea and can help to make it a reality. This helps if complications arise, especially if you want a particular individual on your team, but that individual's supervisor says "no." You need to try to find out the reason for this decision. Your supervisor may be able to help you convince the other supervisor. Remember, moving someone from his permanent assignment, even for a short time, means that a supervisor may need to set new priorities. Unless it is possible for work to remain undone during the course of your project, this means that existing tasks will have to be reassigned to other employees. This is especially true if you are forming a cross-departmental team. The effect on the organization's current priorities and the disruption caused by temporarily shelving tasks or reassigning them means that your supervisor or someone else with the appropriate authority has to make those decisions. It means being adept in working through your organization's internal political process.

It is not always possible to find team members within the organization. The options for obtaining team members from outside of the library range from soliciting unpaid volunteers to hiring contract employees. Short-term contract employees can be hired at a variety of levels, from support staff through professional librarian. If your idea works out, you can request to make the positions permanent, or, in the case of revenue-generating ideas, the lines might be kept on a revenue-dependent basis.

Another source of team members can be external partnerships. These may involve other areas of a school, university, municipal government, vendors (be careful of conflicts of interest), or other member institutions in a library consortium. While it may be obvious that certain projects can and do benefit multiple institutions and provide benefits to your library while opening new markets for a company would benefit by having participants from multiple organizations, smaller projects may also be appropriate since we all face similar issues. Having a team member from another library can both bring a fresh perspective and enable the development of a solution that could benefit multiple libraries.

You may also be able to find a library science student who is interested in serving in a practicum or in working on a project as part of a capstone class. The hours that will be available will be much less than those available if you are hiring the student as a temporary employee, but the student will be working for a grade rather than for cash, which can be very helpful if resources are extremely limited.

Another source of short-term employees is the student worker. These are often people who have had a number of college-level courses in pertinent areas and are professionals-in-training. The use of graduate students can provide a high level of knowledge, and sometimes applicable experience, at a fairly low price. Many university libraries hire graduate library assistants for short-term assignments. These are students in graduate library science programs who have taken specialized coursework and often have worked in libraries. Besides a wage, students gain valuable pre-professional experience that can give them a powerful advantage when later searching for a professional position. High-quality student employees can also be a great source of future librarians for the profession. Regardless of the type of library in which you work, library schools will happily help you to identify and hire students from their programs.

Don't stop at library school students. Many potentially valuable intrapreneurship projects in libraries involve professional skill sets which lie outside of library or information science. Students with coursework or expertise in information technology, graphic arts, history, or many other disciplines could be extremely useful to your project and could be hired in a number of different capacities. Efforts that at first glance appear to be unrelated to the library may in fact be effective marketing and public relations efforts (see Figure 7.2).

Assigning Roles and Responsibilities

The team members have accepted the challenge, and you are ready to work through the internal structure. Since the team has been given the freedom, along with the responsibility, of completing a project, assigning roles and responsibilities to each team member is crucial and should be based on each individual's expertise and experience. Refer back to the BOSI challenge to help define each person. Talk through the innovator's plan. You may find several of your team members have hidden talents, which will help make the project a great success. Consider and define the following roles of

Convertibles ready for action.

Being an intrapreneur means being able to think outside of the box, that is, having the imagination and vision to see the potential relationships and synergies between various people and things that may seem to be unrelated at first glance.

Try this group of puzzle pieces: a library friends' group, a radio station, their parent university, roller derby players, sports cars, custom hot rods, an on-campus church group, a car club, an automotive writer for a magazine, and various local charities. Put it all together and you get the Friends of the W. Frank Steely Library/WNKU Road Rally and Car Show.

Remember that you should always look for as many benefits and beneficiaries as possible. The road rally event began as a fund-raiser/friendraiser for the library's friends group and radio station WNKU. Using that as a central purpose, other groups contributed and benefited from the event. The radio station broadcast from the event, increasing its impact. The university, which contributed its facilities, drew people to the campus, gaining very positive exposure. The church group used its facility to provide food service to the attendees and gained positive exposure. The local charities were invited to exhibit at the car show, giving them exposure to a new public while also increasing excitement and traffic to the overall event. The roller derby players got good PR for their team and added to the atmosphere of the event. In essence, all contributed to the energy and excitement of the event, and all benefited.

The rally itself was based on a historical theme, taking people on a route that highlighted various places that were important to the history and heritage of the region.

Look for the hidden synergies when considering projects with new partners. One of the great ancillary benefits for the library was the result of the fact that few people associate hot rods and roller derby with libraries. The resulting images have been attention-getters for the library and have been used in a number of presentations and materials.

An event of this type also points out the need for intrapreneurs to have the ability to accept a prudent level of risk. A risk-averse person would probably never have taken on a project of this type, after all, cars and libraries? Where's the connection, naysayers ask? By identifying benefits and seeking synergistic partnerships, risk was minimized and potential benefit was maximized.

Figure 7.2: Change Agents in Action

individuals, who all work together toward the goal of implementing the intrapreneur's idea:

- Team leader: A role often taken by the intrapreneur who facilitates meetings, establishes the timeline for success based on her innovator's plan, and recruits team members. The leader keeps the team members excited about the project.

- Team administrator/manager: Serves as a liaison between the project team and the administration and takes care of the team organizationally so that the team is free to complete its assigned task.

- Team secretary: Records key points for progress reports, which are presented to the administration and fellow employees and are highlighted through Web sites, newsletters, and the like. This team member keeps everyone in the organization appraised of progress.

- Timekeeper: Sets up meetings, keeps meetings on track, and issues agendas as needed.

- Specialists: Address the technology, logistics, marketing, and PR requirements, and others as needed.

- Innovators at large: Like specialists, these individuals devote their talents and ideas to the project.

Managing the Team

Once the team is established, set the timeline for implementation with mutually agreed upon milestones and deliverable dates. Clarify interrelationships between team members, volunteers, the community, and others in the organization. Explain, set, and communicate goals to the team and to the organization. Make sure everyone is on board with the idea. Be sure to measure and report progress. Formalize this task so that your accomplishments can be highlights and serve as an inspiration to the team and the organization as a whole. Let people know who is accountable and invite feedback.

Teams are a great idea, but what if you alone are the team? In smaller organizations, you may be team, sponsor, implementer, and marketer all rolled into one frequently overburdened change agent. Will the lack of a team limit your effectiveness? Not necessarily. In some circumstances, a team of one is sufficient to carry out a small project or to bootstrap[8] an effort. In other cases, the creative intrapreneur works to build partnerships both within and outside of the library, institution, or organization. Actively seek out those with the skills or resources to help. Are there things that you can trade for support? If looking outside of the organization, can you obtain volunteer labor to help realize your idea? Are there local businesses, schools, government agencies, or non-profits with which you can collaborate? Intrapreneurship is a creative art, and the successful intrapreneur must be willing at times to develop creative methods for obtaining necessary resources.

Managing the Project

Once the team is established, the focus changes to managing the project. This includes setting a schedule for necessary tasks, a target date for completion of the project, and a marketing plan. Sometimes, the implementation team requires a different set of skills from the idea generation team although all individuals must work together for a common goal; each person must remain flexible and be able to react quickly while working compatibly. All should share the common goal of the successful implementation of the idea. The next chapter will describe the steps involved in managing the project to completion.

Notes

1. Anis Bedda, "Forget Super Heroes—Intrapreneurship Is a Team Sport," *Innovation, Intrapreneurship Conference, Leadership, News*, 2013, http://www.intrapreneurshipconference.com/forget-super-heroes-intrapreneurship-is-a-team-sport/. The Intrapreneurship Conference has been an international event since it was first held in Brussels in 2011. The 7th annual conference met in Munich, Germany, in 2016. The goal of each conference is to "to help corporate innovators driving intrapreneurship by hosting events in locations all around the globe, offering them best content and access to a tribe of entrepreneurial leaders they don't find at their own organizations," http://www.intrapreneurshipconference.com/.
2. Kevin C. DeSouza, *Intrapreneurship: Managing Ideas within Your Organization* (Toronto: University of Toronto Press, 2011), 215.
3. Rich Karlgaard, "Why Small Teams Win: Eight Reasons to Stick to the 'Two-Pizza' Rule," *Young Upstarts, Voice of a New Generation*, April 14, 2014, http://www.youngupstarts.com/2014/04/14/why-small-teams-win-eight-reasons-to-stick-to-the-two-pizza-rule/.
4. It is also important to be aware of overtime laws, both at the state and federal levels. If the team meets during working hours, interested employees, in some cases, may even be denied the opportunity to work additional hours because of labor laws governing overtime compensation. A discussion of overtime pay and compensatory leave is beyond the scope of this book. Be aware that federal and state laws may dictate how many hours

an employee may work. See the US Department of Labor Web site (http:// www.dol.gov/whd/overtime_pay.htm) as well as your organization's human resources department for more information.

5. Alan Deutschman, "Inside the Mind of Jeff Bezos and His Plans for Amazon," *Fast Company*, August 2004, http://www.fastcompany.com/50661/ inside-mind-jeff-bezos.

6. Robert B. Tucker, "Eight Essentials of a Winning Innovation Team," *Innovation Excellence*, March 5, 2015, http://www.innovationexcellence.com/ blog/2015/03/05/eight-essentials-of-a-winning-innovation-team/.

7. BOSI, "What Is Your Entrepreneurial DNA?" https://www.bosidna.com/.

8. *Bootstrapping* is a term used in both entrepreneurial and intrapreneurial activities that simply means that an innovative idea may begin with little or no capital or other resources. It is a way to start small while thinking big and to promote an idea on the proverbial shoestring in terms of resources. One definition reads: "Building a business out of very little or virtually nothing." "Bootstrapping," *BusinessDictionary.com*, http://www.business dictionary.com/definition/bootstrapping.html#ixzz48R2U8htf. In terms of intrapreneurship, it means that the intrapreneur begins with only his idea and time.

Implementation: The Idea Ascendant

> Project management is the process of organizing the way that changes are implemented efficiently within an organization. . . . Often, projects have a finite length, involve a number of activities and people, and have deadlines and fixed budgets. Project managers plan and monitor these, and take corrective action when appropriate.
>
> —Mind Tools[1]

You have sold the value of your idea to your boss, colleagues, and clientele and have received permission to move ahead. You are fortunate enough to have resources, such as employees, and a budget to allow your project to advance. You conducted a pilot project and surveyed your clientele about it. The response was favorable. You received a green light and assembled a team. You are now ready to put your idea into operation. What comes next?

Managing the Project

> Lesson number one: Intrapreneurism must be managed—Promoting intrapreneurism without a direction is like a loose cannon on deck: you can't predict the outcome but someone is bound to get hurt.
>
> —Hitchcock[2]

This is the point in your project where *the rubber meets the road*. You will now take your innovator's plan, develop a step-by-step process to organize it, set deadlines, and manage the process to completion. If you are successful, the result will be the effective delivery of a new service and happy users. If you fail, the hoped-for result becomes a learning experience and an opportunity to refine the idea and try again.

To properly manage your project, your team develops a task schedule and a budget if one is needed. Keep in mind that even if you are not making expenditures, keeping track of staff time spent on the project is still a good idea. You should be able to take much of this directly from your innovator's plan. Try thinking like an administrator and see the big picture for your project and your team while remembering that all of you are responsible for the project's success.

One way to begin is by identifying key tasks needed to implement the project. Is there a specific order in which they must be done? If so, list the tasks as steps, estimate the time needed to complete each one, and then place each step in its appropriate order, tied to a deadline.

Establish milestones. Can some tasks be accomplished simultaneously? Must others take place in a sequence? Charting tasks on a timeline can help to make it easier for team members to understand. In addition, establish key milestones to show the project's progress. This can be easily done using a spreadsheet or word processing document. Use the innovation project worksheet in Figure 8.1 as a starting point, but be sure to keep it flexible and evaluate which deadlines are set in stone and which can slip at bit. Organization and order are great, but, on the other hand, flexibility allows you to seize opportunities that appear outside of the timeline that may allow the project to move forward more quickly. Do not assume that just because this plan is set that the project, and everyone working in it, will stay on task. Don't stick with the ordered plan just because it is a plan: results don't always turn out according to plan. Don't be swamped or drowned by the plan. As Gifford Pinchot noted, "Many organizations have difficulty managing innovation because they insist on an orderly world in which results turn out exactly as planned."[3] Of course, as librarians, we like to have everything in order because it's part of our DNA. On the other hand, a bit of risk once in a while can be beneficial. Modify the innovation project worksheet (Figure 8.1) to outline your plans.

That said, for medium to large projects that would benefit from a more formal, yet still flexible, approach, consider a Gantt chart. Gantt charting represents one very effective way in which project schedules can be placed within a timeline. If you feel like you are juggling 15 balls in the air at one time, taking a bit of time to create a Gantt chart can help you out. Gantt charts show tasks in a visual timeline and give you a concise and complete overview of the project at a glance. You can see what has been accomplished, the progression of tasks, and those still needing work shown against your timeline.

Project title: _____

Project team members: _____

Project leader: _____

Start date: _____

Roll-out date: _____

Evaluation date: _____

Add specific dates to week blocks and times as needed. Add or delete weeks as needed.

	Mon	Tue	Wed	Thur	Fri
Week 1		Team formed	Team meeting: assign roles	Team leader meet with sponsor/ administrator	Set timeline for implementation
Week 2		First Milestone— describe team assignments			
Week 3		Second Milestone— describe			
Week 4					
Week 5					
Week 6		Roll-out week!			
Week 7		Celebrate! Promote!			

Figure 8.1: Innovation Project Worksheet

The Gantt chart shows you

- the timeline for the project in days, weeks, or months, depending upon the length of the project;

- when the project starts and when it should end with full implementation;

- the specific steps or activities to accomplish the project goals;

- when each step begins and ends, indicating how long each should last;
- where one step or activity begins only after another step or activity ends;
- where and when steps or activities overlap with others;
- the date the activities will end and the project will be implemented.

The Gantt chart has been an effective project management tool since the concept was devised concurrently in Poland and the United States. Around 1896, Karol Adamiecki, a Polish engineer working in a steel plant, created a visual management chart, which he called a *harmonogram*. Not long after, around 1910, Henry Gantt, a management consultant and engineer, designed another task-to-time-related chart, which became known by his name as the Gantt chart. Charts were originally written out by hand, but today there are numerous ways to create a simple, useful, and effective chart.

You can create a Gantt chart by hand using graph paper, ruler, and pencil. Or, you can create one on your computer. If you have one of the latest versions of Microsoft Excel you can download a free Gantt template. If you have a more detailed project, you may want to look at the GanttProject (www.ganttproject.biz). This Web site provides a free project management app, which allows you to create Gantt charts, manage resources, and export data to commercial project management software, such as Microsoft Project. Aceproject.com offers an online project management tool at various price points, based on the complexity of your needs. Ranging from free to $99 per month, the product allows you to schedule and manage resources. Microsoft Project (www.microsoft.com) is a commercial product that provides powerful project management capabilities, including the ability to create Gantt charts, timelines, and project budgets. Figure 8.2 demonstrates how to set up your visual timeline.

Whatever method you select, establish realistic boundaries and determine the scope of the project up front. Be sure to set a clear timeline with benchmarks and milestones for each critical task. Track the project and monitor to ensure that tasks are being completed on schedule. While some slippage is inevitable, every effort should be made to keep the project on schedule. The team needs to understand and to help set the parameters while the administration must be kept informed as the project proceeds. This helps to ensure that the project will be completed in a reasonable time and within budget.

What if your well-thought-out timetable starts to slip? One common barrier facing many implementation projects occurs when the process

Add or delete steps and months as needed.

Step Name	Year								
	Month	Month	Month	Month	Month	Month	Month	Month	Month
Step 1	██████████████								
Step 2			████████████████						
Step 3				████████████████					

Step Name	Month								
	Week	Week	Week	Week	Week	Week	Week	Week	Week
Step 1	██████████████								
Step 2			████████████████						
Step 3				████████████████					

Step Name	Week				
	Monday	Tuesday	Wednesday	Thursday	Friday
Step 1	████████████				
Step 2		████████████			
Step 3			████████████		

Figure 8.2: Simple Gantt Chart

dominates the idea and the implementation process becomes too complex. Your team needs to remain focused on the idea and not spend its time writing detailed procedures or worrying about *what-if* scenarios. It is the job of everyone on the team, but especially the team leader, to keep the team on track. If the team continues to miss deadlines it is time to analyze the situation and determine what circumstances seem to be derailing the team. Examples follow:

- A team member falls ill and is out of work for an extended period.
  - Solution: replace the member with another team member or find a new person who is willing to take on the responsibilities.
- A team member becomes stubborn and won't give up an idea modification even after numerous discussions.
  - Solution: replace this member if he cannot be convinced.
- A team member decides that she does not have time for the project because her supervisor just handed her another project and was told to get it done now!
  - Solution: coordinate with administration to release the member from the additional work. If the other project now must take precedence, find a replacement member or redistribute the task.

- A person, department, or administrator who does not believe in the project pushes back and is initiating negativity in the organization.

  - Solution: Personally meet with the individual or group and try to determine exactly why they are objecting to the project. Explain the project and ask for their help and support. If they continue to object, then you simply may have to ignore them.

- One or several team members have bad chemistry that causes conflict and threatens to stifle the innovation.

  - Solution: Have the members talk with each other to try and resolve issues; bring in a third-party member to facilitate a discussion. Try to establish a win-win, rather than an us-versus-them solution. If the conflict persists, then reestablish the team.

At all stages step back and reassess. Consider an off-site meeting or retreat where you can get away from the everyday grind. Have the team rate itself and its accomplishments weekly. Team members should always keep in mind the benefits that the successful implementation of the project will bring their clientele rather than focus on what the team is offering. Analyze your clients' position to understand just how they will view the team's efforts. As Atticus Finch in Harper Lee's award-winning novel *To Kill a Mockingbird* sagely advised his daughter, Scout, "You never really understand a person until you consider things from his point of view . . . until you climb into his skin and walk around in it."[4] Part of understanding the big picture as well as the planning process is understanding failure. *Failure* is not a dirty word, or at least it should not be. Sometimes, a project does not meet the goals and objectives that were established at the beginning. In this case, your evaluation is crucial and should point out where adjustments could have been made and whether one idea turned into another. That is not failure; that is alternate success. If the project does not get completed or is derailed or dies under its own weight, consider that as an opportunity for a new or different innovation. Never stop finding the courage to succeed, and embrace honest feedback. If you, the intrapreneur, intend to be intrapreneurial more than once—and you should—taking these steps will help to preserve and even increase your credibility with your colleagues and your administrators, making it more likely that support for future projects will be forthcoming.

Analyzing Failure

Failure should not just be tolerated, it should be celebrated. Our fear of failure can lead us to pick things to death, to eschew the great for the perfect, and to hesitate to pull the trigger on an idea because we have not created a contingency for every possible problem—no matter how remote the chance of it occurring might actually be.

—John Spears[5]

Experience is the name everyone gives to their mistakes.

—Oscar Wilde[6]

The possibility of failure is a fact of life for intrapreneurs. According to census data, only 47 percent of small businesses started in 2005 were in existence five years later.[7] Similarly, a great many ideas implemented within libraries will not meet the newly established need, will not produce results commensurate with resources required, will meet strong resistance on the part of employees, or will be totally ignored by its target audience. Other projects will die due to a lack of resources. Some will be killed outright by budget cuts. When something fails, an evaluation of the reasons for the failure is essential to not making the same mistake a second time. What about the fact that the project was more costly than anticipated? Why did it not attract users? What might have been done differently? Certainly you do not want to fall into the trap of never trying again. An intrapreneur is always a risk taker who must overcome any concomitant fear of failure that will prevent an idea from being seriously considered. The intrapreneur must acknowledge and overcome the low tolerance for risk inherent among one's colleagues and administrators.

Aversion to imprudent risk is a normal part of the process of good stewardship. All managers and employees should prudently manage the resources provided to them. Since libraries are generally non-profit or government entities that depend on monies from donations or the public purse, librarians are required by law and organizational policy to protect and wisely expend the resources entrusted to them. However, it is proper and desirable to take calculated, or prudent, risks based on the information found in this book. That is, you seek information on needs and perceptions in the form of user feedback and focus group sessions. You tie potential innovations to your strategic plan. You work with your manager and your team to ensure that an innovation is sustainable. In the end, you work to ensure that you are taking *prudent* risk.

Success can never be guaranteed, but you can plan at a prudent level of risk. As John Spears points out in the quote which appears at the head of this section, failure should not just be tolerated, it should be embraced. While you strive to succeed, failure is always a possibility.

However, persons who refuse to accept some risk of failure place many potentially beneficial projects off limits, which leads to a perpetuation of the status quo. They never have an opportunity to learn from their failures.

Hopefully, your manager lets you know that you will not face negative consequences as the result of failure, provided that steps have been taken to limit risks to a prudent level. As an intrapreneur/innovator, you will work with your peers and build a project with a prudent level of risk. This must be factored into the implementation timeline. Make sure to encourage efficient, effective, and timely use of resources. If the project ultimately does fail, then it is time to reevaluate. Take all the information gathered, evaluate it, and go back to square one: idea generation.

Leading Change: Protecting the Implementation and Removing Barriers

Encouraging people to embrace risk and to embrace change requires good leadership and good creativity. You and your team work to communicate the importance of the project to the entire organization throughout the project.

If you encounter barriers after the team has established milestones and deliverable dates, you must be able to communicate clearly why this is happening with the administration and provide alternatives to be implemented to keep the project on course. Each barrier must be fully defined by the team so that you can show exactly why it is a barrier and the impact of that barrier on the project. Will the implementation break down if the barrier remains in place? What is the nature of the barrier? Is the barrier an individual who is not able to carry out the assignment? The team must be able to evaluate the threat and take appropriate action to protect the project, or the threat must be explained to someone who can make the change.

As part of the process, you as an intrapreneur have some questions to answer:

- Are you failing in your assignments? Should you step down?
- How are you evaluating the project?

- How are you reporting progress?
- Are you adhering to deadlines?
- How are you communicating progress?
- If your team is becoming dysfunctional, should you dissolve the team and the project or should you just assemble a new team?

Perhaps one of the most insidious forms of implementation failure stems from burnout from the pressure of keeping a project on target in the face of myriad obstacles. Again, it is the team that deals with these issues and tries to find solutions. Barriers of all kinds must be dealt with in order for the idea to achieve its full implementation.

Celebrating Achievement

After the trials and tribulations, after the implementation of the project, after all the hours and details, after the ups and downs, take the time to celebrate the success of the innovation. However long or short the process, however difficult or easy the steps, this project is ultimately satisfying because it has resulted in an improvement, a change for the better. Shamelessly flaunt the project and tout those people who were supportive or active in its success by letting them know how much they are valued. Advertise to as wide an audience as possible and share the success with others. Consider scheduling an open house or a reception. Invite the public, your colleagues, and the local media. If the media is not able to attend, send a press release, post on Facebook or tweet; use social media to its fullest potential to celebrate this accomplishment as well as call attention to the innovation, what it can offer, what issues it solves, and how it makes lives better.

Many projects, especially any that have had outside funding, usually require some report on the outcomes of the project. This report is the basic information about the project from its inception to goals to an analysis of outcomes along the way with a final summative evaluation. You can easily use these facts and figures to advertise the project and publish in professional journals. Consider submitting the project to *Library Journal*'s Movers and Shakers award.

Sharing project success through presentations in your local community, whether it your innovation is a university event, a public library program, a local service organization meeting (such as Rotary or the

Lions), or for a group of educators, stimulates positive feedback for the library. It allows a wider audience to appreciate both the services the library currently provides along with the new innovation. Public exposure to library services can only increase interest in existing programs.

As library professionals, we also have a responsibility to help to improve the state of professional best practice. This is done through professional dissemination, generally by publishing the results in professional journals and by presenting at professional conferences. As was the case in an earlier chapter, when we discussed searching for as many benefits as possible accruing to as many constituencies as possible, a little thought will make apparent multiple opportunities for presenting the results of your project to interested professionals. In the case of projects involving multiple types of professionals (e.g., librarians, IT professionals, educators, urban planners), opportunities abound to reach various audiences in the form of group presentations targeted to the professional organizations tied to these professions. Effective dissemination increases the impact of your innovation by spreading it to others facing similar problems and stimulates others to carry your idea even further. If you fall into the trap of feeling too busy to write or present, or too modest, or feel that dissemination is unimportant, you risk limiting the effects of what could be a valuable innovation to a very localized audience, depriving untold others of its benefits.

Finally, as part of this celebration, be sure to market the innovation. Marketing is really a communications process. As Rhonda Abrams notes, "There's a common misconception that marketing equals advertising. But marketing is much more than that. Simply stated, marketing is made up of the full range of a company's activities aimed at reaching and motivating customers."[8] In fact, you have been using marketing techniques all along the process: determining a need, generating an idea, distilling the idea, pitching the idea to the library's administration, assembling a team, implementing, and celebrating. In order for your innovation to have a full chance to succeed, you will also need to promote it to its intended users. People cannot use what they do not know about.

This dissemination process may be assigned to the innovative team, a separate marketing group either within or outside of the organization, or become the sole responsibility of the intrapreneur. Even with the predominance of inexpensive digital tools, which can make marketing a less expensive proposition, getting the word out can still remain a daunting task. Consult a variety of marketing toolkits available online to help you get started.

As a further part of the innovative process, be sure to set up a method to capture feedback because you not only have to get the word out, but you have to discover whether the innovation is really working. Consider the American Marketing Association's (AMA's) definition of marketing: "the activity, set of institutions, and process for creating, communicating, delivering, and exchanging offerings that have value for customers, clients, partners, and society at large."[9] Marketing for non-profits is just as important as that for profit-seeking enterprises even though most of us probably think of marketing in terms of convincing someone to buy our product or service, which is certainly an exchange of value (money) for value (the benefit of the product or service). In fact, the AMA's definition goes much further and fits well in the library intrapreneurial context. Marketing, properly realized, is a two-way communication process, allowing us to determine user needs in order to devise a solution, build awareness among various constituencies, encourage use, and obtain feedback to determine the perceived value of the product or service among users and to allow further refinement and development of it. Feedback is crucial to the innovative process, as illustrated in Figure 8.3.

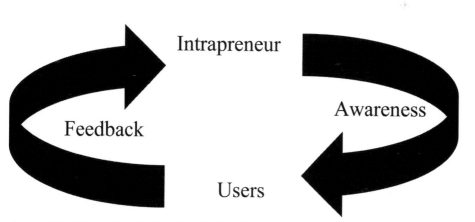

Figure 8.3: Celebration Market: Ask for Feedback

Notes

1. Mind Tools Editorial Team, "What Is Project Management? Managing Complex Tasks and People," *Mind Tools*, 2016, https://www.mindtools.com/pages/article/newPPM_00.htm.
2. Darcy E. Hitchcock, "What Will We Find in an Intrapreneur's Rabbit Hole?" *The Journal for Quality and Participation* 16, no. 7 (12, 1993): 52, http://proxy1.nku.edu/login?url=http://search.proquest.com/docview/219116374?accountid=12817.
3. Gifford Pinchot and Ron Pellman, *Intrapreneuring in Action: A Handbook for Business Innovation* (San Francisco: Berrett-Koehler, 1999): 13.
4. Harper Lee, *To Kill a Mockingbird* (New York: Popular Library, 1962), 34.
5. John Spears, "The Pitfalls of Innovation," *Public Libraries* 53, no. 4 (2014): 26.
6. Oscar Wilde, *Lady Windermere's Fan* (1892) Act III. https://books.google.com/books?id=NqAbCwAAQBAJ&lpg=PP1&dq=Oscar%20Wilde%2C%20Lady%20Windermere%E2%80%99s%20Fan%2C%20(1892)%2C%20Act%20III.&pg=PT58#v=onepage&q=experience&f=false (unpaginated)
7. Scott Shane, "Startup Failure Rates: The Definitive Numbers," *Small Business Trends* (2012), http://smallbiztrends.com/2012/12/start-up-failure-rates-the-definitive-numbers.html.
8. Rhonda Abrams with Julie Vallone, *Successful Marketing: Secrets & Strategies* (Palo Alto, CA: The Planning Shop, 2008), 5.

CHAPTER 9

Completion to New Beginnings

If you don't like something, change it. If you can't change it, change your attitude. Don't complain.

—Maya Angelou[1]

You are an intrapreneur who saw a need, developed and shepherded an idea through to completion and established yourself as a person who has the ability to accept risk and promote change. You have successfully proposed, justified, and sold your idea and have received agreement to put it into operation. You have put together a team, have created a schedule and budget, and have implemented it. You have evaluated all along the way, you have fixed challenges, and your program is operating smoothly. You have celebrated your success. You have shared your project with others, and you are eager to begin a new venture.

One way to start is to go through the steps you used to successfully complete your innovation. With your reputation as a can-do person, you should be able to readily establish the resources and support for a new venture. Use your experience to inspire others in the innovative process. Become the person who assists other change agents to put forward their ideas and become successful. Sometimes, you may also have to reassess what went wrong and how best to make changes or, in comes cases, drop the innovation entirely and start with a fresh idea. This too is part of the learning and innovation process. In all cases, keep these frequently contradictory mantras in mind as you determine which new challenge to undertake:

- Remain optimistic and open to new ideas: even as you are making change, be willing to accept changes to your ideas—do not be stubborn.

- Focus on the big picture and the key components; do not bog down in details and focus on minutiae.

- Concentrate on getting the project done and work with a timeline that moves the project forward, but do not chisel the timeline's goals in stone; remain flexible. Do not manage the project to death and interject more bureaucratic controls—there are enough of those already inherent. Do not satisfice,[2] that is, do not accept an inferior product or implementation idea over a more optimal solution when you know that an alternative method is clearly superior. On the other hand, do not let *perfect* get in to the way of *good*. Implement in a timely manner and keep in mind the costs, as shown in Figure 9.1.

When perfect gets in the way of implementing good, costs go up while quality remains static.

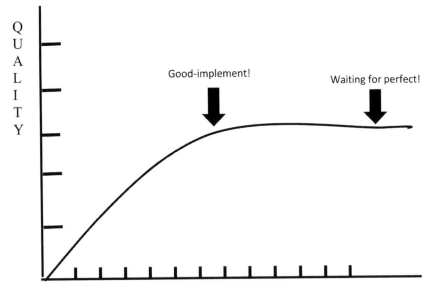

Time + costs (staff time) + impact on user interest

Figure 9.1: Value/Quality/Time Graph

- Win over those who disagree with the innovation, but don't waste too much time on those who simply refuse to recognize or support it. Accept the fact that there will always be naysayers! Move ahead even if it has to be in pieces and takes time and necessitates overcoming opposition. Allow your team the freedom to fully support the project, avoid micromanaging either the team or the project. Be open to allowing others to submit and expand their ideas as part of the innovative process.

- Remain positive and figure out ways around barriers that may develop during the course of implementation and even after.

- Learn and continually think of new ideas, new ways of doing things, ways to expand, and yes even contract, services, all while supporting your organization's mission and your clientele's needs.

- Never forget that is better to go down in flames than not to have tried at all—approach change with gusto, passion, and enthusiasm. *Failure* is just another word for *try again*! Consider the anonymous saying: "You only start failing when you stop trying." Or consider your inspiration to promote change and create useful innovation in the context of these famous lines from the poem *In Memoriam A.H.H.* by Lord Alfred Tennyson:

I hold it true, whate'er befall;

I feel it when I sorrow most;

'Tis better to have loved and lost

Than never to have loved at all.

- Never take a "no" personally. It is not all about you!

- Jump right back into the boiling cauldron and reject lukewarm or ersatz intrapreneurs. Remember that even while you will frequently succeed, you can fail, and sometimes even cause your own failure. The mark of a true change agent is to jump right back into the pot and never stop trying. After all, if no one pushes back at your innovation, then maybe your idea wasn't that interesting to begin with. Make the negative positive.

- Be a team player. You never know how much another person can add to the innovation unless you keep an open mind. Avoid turf battles internally or externally.

- Consider the implications of your innovation through this quote by Herbert S. White, who addressed diverse library clientele and control of library functions between amateurs and professionals: "Librarians . . . particularly in academia, even argue that users know better than we what the library should do, a statement made specious by the recognition that most users do not even know what the library *could* do, only what it does."[3] Did people know they *needed* the iPhone? The Prius?

- Take the innovative risk, but do not expect great financial rewards. Examine and understand your own reward system because as librarians those rewards can exceed anything monetary.

- Finally, be that intrapreneur or change agent. Undertake the task, pursue the idea, create substantive and meaningful change for your organization, your clientele, and your profession.

Congratulations! You are the change agent, intrapreneur, who has worked within an organization to make lives better by providing a new innovation or revising hidebound policies. You have persevered, empowered, and succeeded. You have changed not only your attitude, but the attitudes of others. Continue to be that agent for positive change in your organization.

Notes

1. Maya Angelou, "Maya Angelou Quotes: 15 of the Best," *The Guardian*, May 29, 2014, https://www.theguardian.com/books/2014/may/28/maya-angelou-in-fifteen-quotes.
2. Satisfice is a term developed by 1978 Noble Prize–winning economist Herbert Simon (1916–2001) to describe the human thought process of accepting, and settling for, just good enough. Satisfice is a combination of two words: "satisfy" and "suffice." "Herbert Simon," March 20, 2009, *The Economist*, http://www.economist.com/node/13350892.
3. Herbert S. White, "Entrepreneurship and the Library Profession," *Journal of Library Administration* 8 (1987): 18.

Appendix A: The Intrapreneur Test

Question	Yes	No	Maybe
1. Are you passionate about your library and community? In what ways?			
2. Do you feel that you have the qualifications to suggest, sell, and implement change? (**Sell** is not a bad word. Librarians have to sell their ideas just like anyone else.) List your qualifications.			
3. Have you supported other people's ideas? If *no*, why not? Did you feel that the idea would threaten your position or authority? If *yes*, how did you help that individual to bring his idea to fruition? Did you worry about not getting credit for the idea?			
4. Do you feel that you are too busy to consider new ideas? List the reasons why or why not.			
5. Do you feel stifled in your work environment and powerless to do anything about it? If yes, list reasons why.			
6. Do you consider yourself open to the change that the implementation of your idea might create or to change thrust upon you by someone else's idea? Explain why.			
7. Would you consider your supervisors or managers open to change? Explain why you hold this opinion. Have you ever spoken to them personally about change or innovations?			
8. Are you cautious because you feel that making a mistake could cost you your job? Assess the culture at your organization.			
9. If you are a manager, do you encourage your subordinates to see the big picture as well as to suggest changes? Do you have a process for submitting and evaluating ideas? Do you encourage them when they make suggestions or just shoot them down because you don't have any money or don't want to waste time? List why or why not. Consider whether you, as the manager, are supported by your bosses or the library's organization culture.			
10. If you are an employee, do you randomly blurt out ideas without any additional thought and assume someone else (your manager, your colleagues?) will be the ones to take the time to make it work? Does your library have a process in place for submitting and evaluating ideas?			
11. Do you believe that everyone has the potential to improve the library's internal services and policies?			

(*Continued*)

Question	Yes	No	Maybe

12. Can you handle some ambiguity in your life? Personally? Professionally?

13. Do you consider yourself a disruptive force for good?

14. Are you motivated exclusively by financial rewards?

15. When you have a new idea, do you ask directly, person to person, or indirectly by hinting?

16. Do you handle rejection well?

17. Do you feel that you treat others in a respectful and collegial fashion even when you disagree with them, or do you get irritated, and publicly show it, by their lack of support or understanding?

Consider these rules:

The golden rule: "Do unto others as you would have them do unto you." (Treat others as you yourself would like to be treated.)

The platinum rule: "Do unto others as they want done unto them." (Treat others the way they want to be treated by understanding how others would like to be treated.)

Consider also Rotary International's *four way test* of the things Rotarians think, say, and do. This unwritten code is repeated at each and every Rotary meeting around the world. Rotary is an international service organization and the leading force in the eradication of the poliovirus worldwide.

The Rotary four way test:

1. Is it the truth?

2. Is it fair to all concerned?

3. Will it build goodwill and better friendships?

4. Will it be beneficial to all concerned?

18. Can you embrace a plan with variables and accept ambiguity?

Appendix B: The Intrapreneurship Test—Comments

Question	Yes	No	Maybe
1. Are you passionate about your library and community?	✔		

Clearly the answer is "yes"! The successful intrapreneur wants to advance the organization, thereby better meeting the needs of its clientele. If you don't care, you may be in the wrong organization—or profession. Librarians and people who work in libraries should be passionate about the services their organization can provide.

	Yes	No	Maybe
2. Do you feel that you have the qualifications to suggest, sell, and implement change? (**Sell** is not a bad word. Librarians have to sell their ideas just like anyone else.)	✔		

*Convincing others to agree to an idea of yours that will mean change takes skill, particularly when you are asking someone to contribute resources or to place his own job or reputation on the line. If you do not have the ability, or desire, to make a convincing presentation or **pitch**, you will be severely limited. On the other hand, if you can convince just one other person who is a good **seller**, you have formed a reciprocal partnership that could propel your idea forward.*

	Yes	No	Maybe
3. Have you supported other people's ideas?	✔		

If no, why not? Did you feel that the idea would threaten your position or authority?

If yes, how did you help that individual to bring his idea to fruition? Did you worry about not getting credit for the idea?

When you support others' ideas, they will be more likely to support yours. Be willing to share the credit, and sometimes the risk, and don't be afraid to compromise. Empathize. Consider your perception of your boss. Does she feel threatened by your ideas? How does that affect you? In turn, how does your reaction to others' ideas affect their intrapreneurial zeal? How does it affect your zest for change?

	Yes	No	Maybe
4. Do you feel that you are too busy to consider new ideas?		✔	✔

Ideally: no. Realistically: maybe.

Take stock of your current tasks. We often continue to perform the same tasks long after they have become no longer relevant—or even needed. (Sometimes we just like doing it!) At the same time, we take on (or are forced to take on) new tasks and services. Eventually we become overloaded and are unable to see beyond everyday tasks. For example, some library cataloging units maintained card catalogs alongside their online catalogs for an extended period. What was supposed to save time and labor became additional work. It is difficult to see and develop innovative ideas if you do not take the time to see possibilities. Sometimes you may have an inspiration in the middle of a particularly difficult day and that is the spark for innovation. Avoid saying "I am too tired for that" and "I just don't have the time!"

(Continued)

Question	Yes	No	Maybe
5. Do you feel stifled in your work environment and powerless to do anything about it?		✔	✔

If you answered "yes" to this question, you need to do some deep thinking about your organization and your place within it. Have you made the effort to suggest new services? Were you collegial? Do you need to update or improve your skills and education? You may need to critically examine your own actions/attitudes or, perhaps, move to a different, more nurturing, organization. Sometimes it just takes your time to talk with your bosses.

	Yes	No	Maybe
6. Do you consider yourself open to the change that the implementation of your idea might create or to change thrust upon you by someone else's idea?	✔		

If you answered "no," then you are happy with the status quo and really do not want any changes.

If you answered "yes" you consider yourself open to changes—even if they are disruptive to your regular job duties.

	Yes	No	Maybe
7. Would you consider your supervisors or managers open to change?	✔		✔

Hopefully the answer here is a resounding "Yes!" If not, see if you can determine why. Could a change in your approach help to improve the situation? Remember that persuasion and a collaborative style work as well up the administrative ladder as down.

	Yes	No	Maybe
8. Are you cautious because you feel that making a mistake could cost you your job?		✔	✔

Note that there is a difference between being cautious and being prudent. Nobody wants to lose his job. However, being cautious to the point of paralysis is the antithesis of the intrapreneurial spirit. On the other hand, an unforgiving organizational culture could end your employment. Is being fired the end of the world? Maybe not, but close to it. Obviously this is something to be avoided on all sides. Hiring and training new people is expensive to the organization. You have valuable skills and knowledge. If the worst should happen, remember that you are saleable. Time to become the entrepreneur? Perhaps that innovation you had in mind for your library is the next OCLC or blackboard.

	Yes	No	Maybe
9. If you are a manager, do you encourage your subordinates to see the big picture as well as to suggest changes?	✔		

Hopefully this is a resounding "yes!" Egos play no part when considering the idea. If you feel that change and growth are good, you must support it in others. Encourage your employees when they make suggestions. Avoid the temptation to automatically suppress ideas because you feel that you lack resources or don't want to waste time.

	Yes	No	Maybe
Do you have a process for submitting and evaluating ideas?	✔		

Yes, and if you don't, please create one today. Even if it is only letting your employees know that you can be approached.

Do you encourage them when they make suggestions or just shoot them down because you don't have any money or don't want to waste time?

Question	Yes	No	Maybe

You should encourage and feel encouraged. As a manager or leader, it is your job to provide the opportunities and materials needed to complete tasks. Are grants available? Partnerships?

10. If you are an employee, do you randomly blurt out ideas without any additional thought and assume someone else (your manager, your colleagues?) will be the ones to take the time to make it work?   **No ✔**

Intrapreneurship involves thoughtful consideration of your colleagues' and supervisor's time. Taking time to evaluate your idea and doing some thought as to its operationalization will help ensure that your ideas are taken seriously.

Does your library have a process in place for submitting and evaluating ideas?   **Yes ✔**

Hopefully the answer is "yes!" Why not just ask? Take action, take responsibility!

11. Do you believe that everyone has the potential to improve the library's internal services and policies?   **Yes ✔**

Good ideas are not the exclusive domain of top management. People at all levels have the potential to develop an idea that can benefit the library. In fact, those on the front lines may be uniquely qualified to bring forward ideas for improving or streamlining work flows and may have a better perspective on needed new services. Why not ask about a policy or service that you feel needs to be changed or expanded? Research why a certain structure is in place and then suggest solutions based on the overall administrative goals and the needs of your clientele.

12. Can you handle some ambiguity in your life?   **Yes ✔**

If you cannot, the role of intrapreneur/change agent is probably not for you. Can you embrace a plan with variables? Most experts agree that entrepreneurship is both a science and an art. The science aspect is ordered, is easy to understand, is systematic, embraces rules, and shows quantifiable results. But what about the art aspect? Even with the best planning, your results may mutate daily as you strive toward the best solution. Parts of the concept may have to be changed, adapted, or even removed. Don't fall so in love with your idea that you close your mind to any constructive changes your colleagues may suggest. Invite and listen to comments.

13. Do you consider yourself a disruptive force for good?   **Yes ✔**

*The key phrase here is **disruptive force for good**. What are your intentions? Startups created by entrepreneurs are totally disruptive because of what they are: new, different, bleeding-edge, innovative, unique. Is a disruption really needed for your idea? How disruptive is your idea to the accepted mission of your organization?*

14. Are you motivated exclusively by financial rewards?   **No ✔**

If you are motivated only by financial rewards, you are in the wrong business! The rewards for intrapreneurship are often internal— seeing your idea brought to fruition, improving user services, personal recognition of a job well done.

(Continued)

Question	Yes	No	Maybe
15. When you have a new idea, do you ask directly, person to person, or indirectly by hinting?	✔		

The direct approach generally results in more effective communication of an idea, while also demonstrating that you are invested in it. Starting a whispering campaign to make changes or to foster a personal power play will negatively impact any good ideas you may have.

16. Do you handle rejection well?	✔		✔

New ideas will often get shot down. You may have to bring the idea forward multiple times and do your homework before it stands a chance of acceptance. If you do not handle rejection well, the life of an intrapreneur can be very difficult indeed "No" is not a personal rejection. It may simply mean "not now." While no one likes to be rejected, it's a reminder to practice optimism.

17. Do you feel that you treat others in a respectful and collegial fashion even when you disagree with them, or do you get irritated, and publicly show it, by their lack of support or understanding?	✔		

If you want your ideas to be accepted and to receive support from others, you must treat them with respect. If you undermine colleagues, or try to bully your way through, you will develop a reputation as a backbiter and others will shun you and your ideas— however good they may be!

18. Can you embrace a plan with variables and accept ambiguity?

Librarians and technologists often want to plan everything. Oftentimes this leads to inertia and stagnation. While you do need to have options in place that set budgets, goals, and targets, you do not want to be driven by routine and past failures. Plan for success, not just survival. Remember that neither you nor your plan can be all things to all people.

Index

Page numbers followed by *f* indicate figures.

U

Users, needs assessment, 74, 76

V

Value, 4, 16, 52, 63, 75, 91–92, 93, 142*f*; library services, 4–5, 66; Say's definition, 4

W

Wallas, Graham, 45
Werner, Lance, 75–76

W. Frank Steely Library, Northern Kentucky University (NKU), 26–27, 48, 98n24, 124*f*; IPAC (Intellectual Property Awareness Center), 91
White, Herbert S., 3, 29, 143
Wilde, Oscar, 135

Y

Young Men's Christian Association (YMCA), 6

About the Authors

ARNE J. ALMQUIST is associate provost for learning sciences and technologies and dean of the library at Northern Kentucky University (NKU). Under his leadership, NKU's library has developed very successful undergraduate and continuing education programs in library science and was successful in obtaining two nearly $1 million Institute of Museum and Library Services (IMLS) grants to fund statewide library science education partnerships in Kentucky and West Virginia. He has presented and published on library marketing, entrepreneurship, and implementation of information technology. Almquist holds a doctorate in information science from the University of North Texas.

SHARON G. ALMQUIST teaches as an online adjunct professor at several universities and is currently pursuing a certificate in entrepreneurship at Northern Kentucky University. Previously, she served as head of the media library at the University of North Texas. Her published works include Libraries Unlimited's *Distributed Learning and Virtual Librarianship*; Greenwood's *Opera Mediagraphy: Video Recordings and Motion Pictures* and *Opera Singers in Recital, Concert, and Feature Film: A Mediagraphy*; and *Sound Recordings and the Library*.